Vegetarian
BIBLE

Vegetarian
BIBLE

From the earth to the table

Consultant Editors
Nicola Graimes and Fiona Biggs

Love Food ® is an imprint of Parragon Books Ltd

Parragon
Queen Street House
4 Queen Street
Bath BA1 1HE , UK

ISBN: 978-1-4075-9284-8

Printed in China

Internal Design by Talking Design
Consultant editors Nicola Graimes and Fiona Biggs
Photography by Mike Cooper
Cover photography by Clive Streeter
Home Economy by Lincoln Jefferson
Illustrations by Coral Mula

NOTES FOR THE READER

This book uses imperial, metric, and U.S. cup measurements. Follow the
same units of measurement throughout; do not mix imperial and metric.
All spoon measurements are level: teaspoons are assumed to be 5 ml,
and tablespoons are assumed to be 15 ml. Unless otherwise stated, milk is
assumed to be whole, eggs and individual vegetables, such as potatoes,
are medium, and pepper is freshly ground black pepper.
The times given are an approximate guide only. Preparation times differ
according to the techniques used by different people and the cooking
times may also vary from those given as a result of the type of oven used.
Optional ingredients, variations, or serving suggestions have not been
included in the calculations.
Recipes using raw or very lightly cooked eggs should be avoided by
infants, the elderly, pregnant women, convalescents, and anyone with
a chronic condition. Pregnant and breastfeeding women are advised
to avoid eating peanuts and peanut products. People with nut allergies
should be aware that some of the prepared ingredients used in the
recipes in this book may contain nuts. Always check the packaging before
use. Vegetarians should be aware that some of the prepared ingredients
used in the recipes in this book may contain animal products. Always
check the packaging before use.

CONTENTS

INTRODUCTION 08
WHAT IS A VEGETARIAN? 10
HEALTH BENEFITS 12
THE IMPORTANCE OF A BALANCED DIET 14
ESSENTIAL VITAMINS AND MINERALS 16
PLANNING MEALS 18
TYPES OF VEGETABLES 20
TYPES OF FRUITS 22
TYPES OF GRAINS, CEREALS & BEANS 26
TYPES OF DAIRY PRODUCE 28
HERBS & SPICES 30
ESSENTIAL COOKING TECHNIQUES 32
BASIC RECIPES 36

SHOOTS, ROOTS & STEMS 40
DIRECTORY OF SHOOTS, ROOTS & STEMS 42
SWEET POTATO & APPLE SOUP 44
BEET SALAD 46
POTATO FRITTERS WITH ONION & TOMATO
    RELISH 48
ARTICHOKE & PIMIENTO FLATBREAD 50
POTATO GNOCCHI WITH WALNUT PESTO 52
CARROT & ORANGE STIR-FRY 54
GARLIC MASH POTATOES 56
ROASTED POTATO WEDGES WITH SHALLOTS
    & ROSEMARY 58
CARAMELIZED SWEET POTATOES 60
ROASTED ROOT VEGETABLES 62
BAKED CELERY WITH CREAM 64
ASPARAGUS WITH SWEET TOMATO DRESSING 66
ASPARAGUS & SUN-DRIED TOMATO RISOTTO 68
BEAN SPROUT SALAD 70
STIR-FRIED BEAN SPROUTS 72
FENNEL RISOTTO WITH VODKA 74

FRUITS & SQUASHES 76
DIRECTORY OF FRUITS & SQUASHES 78
AVOCADO & ALMOND SOUP 80
GUACAMOLE 82
CUCUMBER & TOMATO SOUP 84
TOMATO & ROSEMARY FOCACCIA 86
BELL PEPPERS WITH FETA 88
TOMATO & POTATO TORTILLA 90
PASTA SALAD WITH CHARBROILED BELL
    PEPPERS 92
ZUCCHINI & BASIL RISOTTO 94
PASTA ALL'ARRABBIATA 96
CHILI TOFU TORTILLAS 98
PASTA SHAPES WITH PUMPKIN SAUCE 100
PUMPKIN CHESTNUT RISOTTO 102
BUTTERNUT SQUASH STIR-FRY 104
STUFFED EGGPLANTS 106
EGGPLANT CURRY 108
CORNMEAL WITH TOMATOES & GARLIC
    SAUCE 110

MUSHROOMS & THE ONION FAMILY 112

DIRECTORY OF MUSHROOMS & ONIONS 114

CREAMY MUSHROOM & TARRAGON SOUP 116

WILD MUSHROOM BRUSCHETTA 118

MUSHROOM PASTA WITH PORT 120

PARMESAN CHEESE RISOTTO WITH
MUSHROOMS 122

MIXED MUSHROOM PIZZA 124

RED ONION, TOMATO & HERB SALAD 126

FLATBREAD WITH ONION & ROSEMARY 128

CARAMELIZED ONION TART 130

VEGETABLE CAKES 132

ONION DAL 134

LEEK & GOAT CHEESE CRÊPES 136

LEEK & HERB SOUFFLÉS 138

LEEKS WITH YELLOW BEAN SAUCE 140

CHILLED GARLIC SOUP 142

ROAST GARLIC WITH GOAT CHEESE 144

GARLIC SPAGHETTI 146

NUTS, SEEDS & BEANS 148

DIRECTORY OF NUTS & SEEDS 150

DIRECTORY OF BEANS 152

CHILLED PEA SOUP 154

CHICKPEA SOUP 156

HUMMUS TOASTS WITH OLIVES 158

CHICKPEA & VEGETABLE STEW 160

VEGETABLE & BLACK BEAN SPRING ROLLS 162

BEAN BURGERS 164

FAVA BEANS WITH FETA 166

SAUCY BORLOTTI BEANS 168

EGYPTIAN BROWN BEANS 170

KIDNEY BEAN RISOTTO 172

GREEN BEAN SALAD WITH FETA 174

SESAME HOT NOODLES 176

PASTA WITH PESTO 178

NUTTY BLEU CHEESE ROAST 180

CASHEW PAELLA 182

BLEU CHEESE & WALNUT TARTLETS 184

BRASSICAS & LEAVES 186

DIRECTORY OF BRASSICAS & LEAVES 188

BROCCOLI & CHEESE SOUP 190

TRADITIONAL BEAN & CABBAGE SOUP 192

SPINACH & FETA TRIANGLES 194

CAULIFLOWER, BROCCOLI & CASHEW
    SALAD 196

SPINACH LASAGNE 198

STUFFED CABBAGE ROLLS 200

CAULIFLOWER & BROCCOLI TART 202

CAULIFLOWER, EGGPLANT & GREEN
    BEAN KORMA 204

CHILE BROCCOLI PASTA 206

SPINACH & RICOTTA GNOCCHI 208

CABBAGE & WALNUT STIR-FRY 210

BRUSSELS SPROUTS WITH CHESTNUTS 212

WATERCRESS, ZUCCHINI & MINT SALAD 214

BOK CHOY WITH CASHEWS 216

RED CURRY WITH MIXED LEAVES 218

ARUGULA & TOMATO RISOTTO 220

INDEX 222

INTRODUCTION

The *Vegetarian Bible* is a comprehensive guide to preparing, cooking, and serving a vast range of vegetables, beans, nuts, and seeds. The directories at the front of each chapter introduce the fabulous variety of vegetarian food—a far cry from the days when there was very little choice of vegetables available and when vegetarianism was regarded as something of a fad. The recipes in this book, inspired by cuisines of places as diverse as North Africa and China, cater for every meal type and occasion, from quick snacks and dips to hearty main courses, and from delicious salads to hearty meal-in-a-bowl soups.

WHAT IS A VEGETARIAN?

The plant-based vegetarian diet is enjoyed by millions of people around the world, people as diverse as the variety of fruits and vegetables offered at your local store or supermarket.

The most basic definition of a vegetarian is someone who doesn't eat meat, poultry, game, fish, shellfish, or other seafood, or the by-products of slaughter, such as gelatin or animal fats. Most vegetarians choose to get their nutrients from a diet of fruits and vegetables, grains, nuts, beans, and seeds. Some vegetarians also include dairy products and eggs.

While some vegetarians make this choice for ethical and moral reasons and others for religious reasons, many vegetarians simply enjoy the culinary pleasure of eating plenty of flavorsome, fresh vegetables and fruits. Whatever the reasons, however, the popularity of vegetarianism is increasing and no longer carries the stigma of being a weird, alternative lifestyle that it once had in Western countries. And whatever reason you have for wanting vegetarian recipes, you'll find a mouthwatering selection in this collection.

Types of vegetarian
Just as the plant world offers much variety, the vegetarian diet comes in many guises. These are some of the most common vegetarian choices:
Demi-veg For many people, this can be a first step to becoming a vegetarian because the diet eliminates all meat and poultry, but does include seafood.
Fruitarian These vegetarians eat mostly raw fruits, grains, and nuts, in the belief that only plant foods that can be harvested without killing a plant should be eaten.
Lacto-vegetarian Dairy products, but no eggs, are included in this diet. This style of vegetarianism provides a lot of culinary scope in the kitchen because it includes cheese, cream, milk, and yogurt.
Lacto-ovo-vegetarian Dairy products and eggs are included in this diet, providing great variety at mealtimes. This is the most common form of vegetarianism and all the recipes in this book are suitable for this lifestyle.
Macrobiotic vegetarian This diet is usually followed for spiritual and philosophical reasons. It maintains a balance between foods seen as yin (positive) and yang (negative).
Vegan This is a vegetarian whose daily diet doesn't include any dairy products or eggs. Although many millions of people around the world are vegan, this isn't always the straightforward choice it appears to be. Vegans must become diligent label readers to avoid the less-than-obvious butter and eggs in many prepared foods. One reason Asian stir-fries and stews are so popular with vegans is because the staple rice and mung-bean noodles are not made with eggs, as Italian pasta is.

Becoming a vegetarian
If you are new to eating a meatless diet, it can be comforting to know that many familiar, everyday dishes are, in fact, vegetarian, especially if you decide to adopt a lacto-ovo diet. Write down a list of all your favorite meals and chances are you'll find some that easily fit your new diet—for example, scrambled eggs or broiled cheese sandwiches. You'll find everyday favorites in this global collection of recipes that you might already enjoy eating as an omnivore, such as Pasta Salad with Charbroiled Bell Peppers, Creamy Mushroom & Tarragon Soup, Pasta with Pesto, and Roasted Root Vegetables. Take-out favorites, such as Eggplant Curry and Sesame Hot Noodles, for example, can also feature in vegetarian meals. You will quickly appreciate how old-fashioned the idea is that vegetarians eat only brown rice and salad greens!

If becoming a vegetarian means a radical overhaul of all your cooking and eating habits, make the change gradually. Rather than trying to change a lifetime of eating habits overnight, start by simply cutting out red meat for a couple of weeks, then go on to eliminating fish and shellfish and, finally, poultry. Then you can carry on slowly eliminating dairy products or other foods as you want. This approach will also help you avoid cravings.

Try to cook something new two or three times a week. Highlight recipes in this collection that you've never tried before and you will soon discover how varied and delicious a vegetarian diet can be.

HEALTH BENEFITS

Humans have always eaten plant-based diets and today most of the world's population eats a vegetarian or near-vegetarian diet. Every day more people are adopting a meat-free lifestyle. Many and varied reasons fuel this expansion of vegetarianism around the globe. Religious conviction and the belief that a vegetarian diet is a healthy choice are the deciding factors for many, but for others the conversion to vegetarianism comes from the desire to eat well for less money, concern about the environment, and worries over the more-numerous-than-ever food scares. For many vegetarians, it is, quite simply, an ethical decision not to kill animals.

Whatever your reasons for becoming a vegetarian, you will undoubtedly find that vegetarianism offers great scope and choice at mealtimes. Along with many delicious Western dishes, you'll find inspiration for meals from cultures around the world in the delicious collection of recipes in this book. India and China have large vegetarian populations, but flavorsome recipe ideas from Africa, the rest of Southeast Asia, the Middle East, and the countries bordering the Mediterranean are also included.

Health benefits of going green

One of the great appeals of a vegetarian diet, especially in the West, is that you don't eat any of the saturated fats found in animal products that have been linked with some of the most deadly diseases of the twenty-first century, such as heart disease and various forms of cancer.

Unfortunately, a vegetarian diet in itself won't guarantee optimum health. If you simply replace the meat in your old diet with hard cheese and whole milk, for example, which are both high in saturated fat, you might not see much improvement. And, likewise, if you try to live on a diet of just brown rice, tofu, and bean sprouts you won't be getting the nutrients you need for a healthy body—these are discussed in the following pages.

There is no doubt, however, that a vegetarian diet will go a long way toward meeting today's many nutritional guidelines. As a vegetarian you will almost certainly eat more than the recommended five portions of fruits and vegetables a day, so, if you make smart changes, you should eliminate many of the potential health problems associated with a meat-based diet. A varied vegetarian diet will also be higher in fiber, which is believed to help prevent constipation, bowel disorders, and other serious health problems. Some studies have also determined that obesity, with its numerous health complications, is less of a problem for vegetarians than it is for meat eaters.

Despite all the confusing—and often conflicting—advice about healthy eating, the one thing nutritionists agree on is that eating at least five portions, or 14 oz/ 400 g, of fruits and vegetables every day forms the backbone of a healthy diet. Plant foods are a powerhouse of essential nutrients—these include the B vitamins, especially important for women planning a family; vitamin C, for general immunity and healing; and powerful antioxidants that reduce the risk of heart diseases, cancer, cataracts, arthritis, and sperm damage. Antioxidants also reduce some of the problems associated with aging by fighting free radicals that are caused by pollutants in the environment and as a by-product of natural cell functions. This is why a vegetarian diet can be instrumental in your overall well-being.

A religious choice

Some religions, who believe in reincarnation, are prohibited by their religious beliefs from eating meat. For many vegetarians, avoiding heavy food, such as red meat, is regarded as a step toward spiritual enlightenment. They believe that consuming lighter, less dense food lets an individual reach a higher state of consciousness.

A lifestyle choice

In light of the all-too-frequent health scares, such as those over CJD (Creutzfeldt-Jacob disease), caused by eating meat from cows with BSE (bovine spongiform encephalopathy), and avian flu in poultry, the changeover to a meat-free diet provides peace of mind for many converts to vegetarianism. Vegetarianism is also believed to reduce the likelihood of potentially fatal illness from bacterial infections, such as *E. coli* in meat or salmonella in eggs.

Food hygiene

Eating and cooking with only plant-based ingredients, however, doesn't automatically give you a clean bill of health. Food hygiene is just as important as it is when cooking with animal products. Unless your ingredients are organic, it is advisable to wash them thoroughly before cooking to remove any pesticide residue. You can buy a special solution for washing fruits and vegetables from health-food stores and some supermarkets.

THE IMPORTANCE OF A BALANCED DIET

Vegetarians, just like meat eaters, need a variety of nutrients on a daily basis in order to function in tip-top form and remain healthy. And it is only by eating a wide variety of foods every day that you get all the nutrients you need naturally. If, for example, you eat a selection of green, red, yellow, and orange fruits and vegetables at each meal, you will probably be getting all the essential nutrients. If, however, you look at your plate and see only brown and beige, it is time to rethink your menu planning. Beet Salad, Pasta Shapes with Pumpkin Sauce, Carrot & Orange Stir-Fry, and Sweet Potato & Apple Soup are just a few of the colorful recipes that will help you along the road to healthy eating.

Variety for health

The following food choices are recommended for your daily diet:
- 4–5 servings of fruits and vegetables
- 3–4 servings of cereals and/or grains or potatoes
- 2–3 servings of nuts, seeds, and beans
- 2 servings of milk, cheese, eggs, or soy products
- small amount of vegetable oil, margarine, or butter
- yeast extract, such as Marmite, fortified with vitamin B12

If that looks like a huge amount of food, it isn't. Something as simple and as satisfying as Leek & Goat Cheese Crêpes, for example, provides at least one serving from four of the categories. When you want a snack, try a baked potato topped with grated cheese or a handful of toasted nuts and you'll be well on your way to reaching the daily target.

The goodness in food

All the food you eat contains a combination of proteins, carbohydrates, and fats—you need a balanced mixture of each every day to stay healthy.

Protein, made up of amino acids, is essential for the growth, development, and maintenance and repair of cells. Unfortunately, soy products are the only nonanimal foods that contain all the essential amino acids. That is why it is so important to eat a variety of food every day, although if you include cheese, eggs, cow's milk, and yogurt in your diet you are less at risk of being protein-deficient. Good sources of protein include all soy products, such as tofu, soy milk, and commercial textured vegetable protein, beans, whole grains and cereals, nuts and seeds, and butter, cheese, cow's milk, and eggs.

Carbohydrates give you energy. They can be either simple or complex, and it is the complex carbohydrates that are most nutritionally beneficial, containing a mix of vitamins and minerals and releasing the energy you need slowly, so that you will feel the benefits for longer. Sweet Potato & Apple Soup and Chickpea & Vegetable Stew are examples of delicious dishes that supply generous amounts of complex carbohydrates. Good sources are almost all fruits and vegetables, especially root vegetables, potatoes, and bananas; beans; and whole grains, cereals, and pasta.

What Is a Serving?

- scant ½ cup fruit juice (only one glass a day counts)
- 1 medium fruit or vegetable, such as an apple, orange, or onion
- 3 heaping tablespoons of fresh or canned fruit salad, sliced carrots, or mushrooms or cooked lentils
- 1 tablespoon of raisins or golden raisins, or 4 dried apricots, or a handful of banana chips

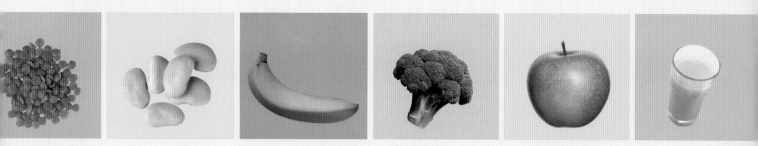

Despite the modern tendency to look at anything labeled "lowfat" as beneficial, a small amount of fat in your diet is needed to feel well and look good. Most of the fat that comes from animal products, however, is saturated and commonly known as the "bad" fat because of the links with serious diseases. "Good" fats, which are called polyunsaturated or monosaturated, come from vegetable plants—for example, olive and sunflower oils, and these are the ones you should use in cooking and salad dressings.

One of the bonuses of eating a vegetarian diet is that most fruits and vegetables are very low in saturated fat, and the high-fat plant foods, such as avocados, olives, nuts, and seeds, contain the "good" fats. Polyunsaturated or monounsaturated fats are those that come from vegetable sources—for example, olive and sunflower oils. Avoid anything with palm oil on the label.

Vitamins for vegans
Anyone adopting a vegan diet should consult a qualified nutritionist or doctor. Vitamin B12, essential for healthy red blood cells, is lacking in a vegan diet. Vegans should consider taking a B12 supplement or eat soy products supplemented with B12.

ESSENTIAL VITAMINS AND MINERALS

VITAMIN/MINERAL	FUNCTION	GOOD VEGETARIAN SOURCES	PROBLEMS CAUSED BY DEFICIENCY
VITAMIN A (retinol in animal foods, beta carotene in plant foods)	For healthy vision, bone growth, skin, and tissue repair. Beta carotene acts as an antioxidant and supports the immune system	Dairy products, egg yolks, margarine, carrots, apricots, squash, red bell peppers, broccoli, green leafy vegetables, mangoes, dried apricots, and sweet potatoes	Poor night vision, dry skin, and impaired immune system, especially respiratory disorders
VITAMIN B1 (thiamine)	Essential for breaking down carbohydrates, protecting the nervous system, muscles, and heart, promoting growth, and boosting mental well-being	Whole grain cereals, brewer's yeast, yeast extract, Brazil nuts, sunflower seeds, peanuts, rice, bran, and mycoprotein (Quorn®)	Depression, irritability, nervous disorders, memory loss; common among alcoholics
VITAMIN B2 (riboflavin)	Essential for energy production, healthy skin, tissue repair, and maintenance	Cheese, eggs, milk, yogurt, fortified breakfast cereals, yeast extract, almonds, whole wheat bread, mushrooms, prunes, cashews, and pumpkin seeds	Lack of energy, skin problems, dry cracked lips, numbness, and itchy eyes
VITAMIN B3 (niacin)	Essential for energy production, healthy digestive system, skin, and nervous system	Beans, yeast extract, potatoes, fortified breakfast cereals, wheat germ, peanuts, cheese, eggs, mushrooms, green leafy vegetables, figs, prunes, and sesame seeds	Deficiency is unusual, but is characterized by lack of energy, depression, and scaly skin
VITAMIN B6 (pyridoxine)	Essential for assimilating protein and fat, red blood cell formation, and a healthy immune system	Eggs, wheat germ, whole wheat flour, yeast extract, breakfast cereals, peanuts, bananas, currants, and lentils	Anemia, dermatitis, and depression
VITAMIN B12 (cyanocobalamin)	Essential for red blood cell formation, growth, healthy nervous system, and energy production	Dairy products, eggs, fortified breakfast cereals, cheese, yeast extract, fortified soy milk	Fatigue, poor resistance to infection, breathlessness, and anemia
Folate (folic acid)	Essential for red blood cell formation, making genetic material (DNA), and protein synthesis. Extra is needed preconception and during pregnancy to protect the fetus against neural tube defects	Green leafy vegetables, broccoli, fortified breakfast cereals, bread, nuts, beans, bananas, yeast extract, and asparagus	Anemia and appetite loss; also linked to neural defects in babies
VITAMIN C (ascorbic acid)	Essential for healthy skin, teeth, bones, gums, immune system, resistance to infection, energy production, and growth	Citrus fruit, melons, strawberries, tomatoes, broccoli, potatoes, bell peppers, and green leafy vegetables	Impaired immune system, fatigue, insomnia, and depression
VITAMIN D	Essential for healthy teeth and bones; aids absorption of calcium and phosphate	Sunlight, nonhydrogenated vegetable margarine, vegetable oils, eggs, and dairy products	Bone and muscle weakness. Long-term shortage results in rickets

VITAMIN/MINERAL	FUNCTION	GOOD VEGETARIAN SOURCES	PROBLEMS CAUSED BY DEFICIENCY
VITAMIN E (tocopherol)	Essential for healthy skin, circulation, and cell maintenance; as an antioxidant, it protects vitamins A and C in the body	Seeds, wheat germ, nuts, vegetable oils, eggs, whole wheat bread, green leafy vegetables, oats, sunflower oil, avocado, and fortified breakfast cereals	Increased risk of heart disease, strokes, and certain cancers
VITAMIN K	Essential for effective blood clotting	Spinach, cabbage, and cauliflower	Deficiency is rare
Calcium	Essential for building and maintaining bones and teeth, muscle function, and the nervous system	Dairy products, green leafy vegetables, sesame seeds, broccoli, dried fruit, beans, almonds, spinach, watercress, and tofu	Soft and brittle bones, osteoporosis, fractures, and muscle weakness
Iron	Essential component of hemoglobin, which transports oxygen in the blood	Egg yolks, fortified breakfast cereals, green leafy vegetables, dried fruit, cashews, beans, whole grains, tofu, pumpkin seeds, molasses, and brown rice	Anemia, fatigue, and low resistance to infection
Magnesium	Essential for healthy muscles, bones, and teeth, normal growth, and energy production	Nuts, seeds, whole grains, beans, tofu, dried figs, dried apricots, and green vegetables	Deficiency rare, but characterized by lethargy, weak bones and muscles, depression, and irritability
Phosphorus	Essential for healthy bones and teeth, muscle function, energy production, and the assimilation of nutrients, particularly calcium	Found in most foods: milk, cheese, yogurt, eggs, nuts, seeds, beans, and whole grains	Deficiency is rare
Potassium	Important in maintaining the body's water balance, normal blood pressure, and nerve transmission	Bananas, milk, beans, nuts, seeds, whole grains, potatoes, fruits, and root vegetables	Weakness, thirst, fatigue, mental confusion, and raised blood pressure
Selenium	Essential for protecting against free radical damage and for red blood cell function as well as healthy hair and skin	Avocados, lentils, milk, cheese, whole wheat bread, cashews, walnuts, seaweed, and sunflower seeds	Reduced immunity
Zinc	Essential for a healthy immune system, tissue formation, normal growth, wound healing, and reproduction	Peanuts, cheese, whole grains, sunflower and pumpkin seeds, beans, milk, hard cheese, yogurt, wheat germ, and mycoprotein (Quorn®)	Impaired growth and development, slow wound healing, and loss of sense of taste and smell

PLANNING MEALS

The key to a good diet is variety—serving the same meals every week will soon dull even the most enthusiastic palate. A balanced meal is one that combines sufficient amounts of protein, carbohydrate, fiber, the right types of fat, vitamins, and minerals. The ideal diet includes enough calories to provide the body with the vital energy it needs, but not an excess, which leads to weight gain.

Keeping a meal balanced

Make sure each meal contains a protein (eggs, beans, tofu, dairy products, nuts, and seeds) and a carbohydrate (pasta, rice, whole grains, bread) element. Despite the current popularity of low-carb diets, it is recommended that at least 50 percent of a meal is carbohydrate based. Remember that many foods, such as beans and whole grains, are a combination of protein and carbohydrate. A moderate amount of fat in the diet is essential, not only for health, but also because it contributes to the taste, texture, and palatability of food. Restrict fat levels to no more than 30 percent of your daily diet and stick to polyunsaturated fats.

Try to include at least two different types of cooked vegetable (steamed, stir-fried, microwaved, or roasted, rather than boiled) in the main meal, or prepare a large salad that combines a range of different types of different-colored vegetables, such as arugula, watercress, spinach, beet, avocado, tomatoes, and carrot. Fruit or fruit-based desserts make a perfect and convenient end to a meal or lowfat snack.

Try not to stick to the same meals every week. Experiment with different foods and try out new recipes. Before you do your weekly shopping, either write down or mentally prepare a week's repertoire of meals. In this way, you can ensure that you eat a range of different foods and that you will have the correct ingredients on hand instead of a collection of foods that do not work together.

It is a common misconception that vegetarians have to combine protein foods meticulously in every meal to achieve the correct balance of amino acids. The latest expert advice states that, provided you eat a varied range of vegetarian protein foods on a daily basis, this is sufficient; therefore, intentionally combining proteins is unnecessary.

Vegetarian Children

There is no reason why children should not thrive on a vegetarian diet—as long as it is not based on cheese sandwiches, beans, and fries. However, they do have slightly different dietary requirements from adults. Young children can find fiber difficult to digest in large amounts; too much can make them feel full before they have been able to ingest enough nutrients and can lead to stomach upsets. Fiber can also interfere with the absorption of iron, zinc, and calcium. Refined bran should not be added to a young child's diet. Reduced-fat foods, such as skim milk and lowfat cheese, lack the much-needed calories, and therefore, energy required by young growing children. Reduced-fat dairy products are suitable for children over five years, but younger children require the whole-fat equivalent. Parents are also advised to give their children at least five portions of fruits and vegetables a day, but this should be divided as three portions of fruits and two of vegetables—fruits provide plenty of energy. Babies and young children do not have the capacity to eat large amounts of food and so need to eat three small nutritious meals a day, plus two healthy snacks.

Watch Out For...

It is always wise to check food and drink labels when shopping. The following checklist makes a useful reference guide.

ADDITIVES
These include emulsifiers, colorings, and flavorings, and may or may not be vegetarian. Two of the most common are E441 (gelatin), a gelling agent derived from animal parts and bones, and E120 (cochineal), made from crushed insects.

ALBUMEN
Albumen may be derived from battery-farmed eggs.

ALCOHOL
Alcohol is clarified using animal ingredients. All cask-conditioned "real" ales, and some bottled, canned, and keg ales are fined (clarified) with isinglass derived from the swim bladders of certain tropical fish. Wine may also be fined with isinglass, dried blood, egg albumen derived from battery hens, gelatin, and chitin from crab and shrimp shells. Vegetarian alternatives include bentonite, kieselguhr, kaolin, and silica gel. Nonvintage port is fined with gelatin.

ANIMAL FATS
Animal fats are sometimes found in cookies, cakes, pie dough, stock, fries, margarine, prepared meals, and ice cream. Edible fats can mean animal fats.

ASPIC
Aspic is a savory jelly derived from meat or fish.

CANDY
Candy may contain gelatin, cochineal, and animal fats.

CHEESE
Many cheeses are produced using animal rennet, an enzyme taken from the stomach of a calf. Vegetarian cheese is made using microbial or fungal enzymes. Nonvegetarian cheese is often used in pesto, sauces, and prepared meals.

EGGS
Eggs are animal products. Some foods, such as mayonnaise or pasta, may contain battery-farmed eggs. If possible, try to buy organic free-range eggs.

GRAVY
Gravy is made from meat juices, although vegetarian gravy mixes do exist.

GELATIN
Desserts made with gelatin usually contain animal-derived gelatin, but it is possible to buy vegetarian alternatives set with agar-agar or guar gum.

MARGARINE
Margarine may contain animal-derived vitamin D3, fats, gelatin, and E numbers as well as whey.

SOFT DRINKS
Soft drinks, particularly canned orange drinks, may contain gelatin, which is used as a carrier for added beta carotene.

SOUP
Soup may contain animal stock or fat.

SUET
Suet is animal fat, but vegetarian versions do exist.

WORCESTERSHIRE SAUCE
Most brands contain anchovies, but vegetarian versions do exist.

YOGURT, CRÈME FRAÎCHE, FROMAGE FRAIS, AND ICE CREAM
Some lowfat varieties may contain gelatin.

TYPES OF VEGETABLES

The mainstays of most vegetarian diets are the colorful, flavorful vegetables that bring variety to every meal. Not only are vegetables packed with vital vitamins and minerals, and plenty of dietary fiber, they are versatile ingredients that can be baked, boiled, stir-fried, broiled, steamed—and even enjoyed raw. There is no reason for a vegetarian meal to be bland or dull!

Shoots, Roots, & Stems

Artichokes Asparagus Bean Sprouts Beets Carrots Fennel Potatoes Sweet Potatoes

When it comes to filling soups, stews, and roasts, few ingredients beat hearty roots and tubers—but roots also make interesting, colorful salads. As well as containing various nutrients, roots are an excellent source of complex carbohydrate, which provides energy throughout the day. Bean sprouts can be used in stir-fries and salads.

Buy dry, firm beets, carrots, fennel, potatoes, and sweet potatoes. Asparagus and celery should be firm and snap easily and crisply. Bean sprouts should be crisp and creamy white in color, without any brown.

Fruits & Squashes

Avocados Bell Peppers Butternut Squash Cucumbers Eggplants Pumpkins Tomatoes Zucchini

The bright and vibrant colors of these vegetables tell you at a glance that they are bursting with goodness. The tomato is actually a fruit, but is treated as a vegetable, and all these ingredients are collectively known as "vegetable fruits," because they carry the seeds of the plant on which they grow. All vegetable fruits can be baked, boiled, roasted, and stir-fried, but avocados, zucchini, bell peppers, and tomatoes also make excellent, healthy salads when eaten raw.

When shopping, look for plump, firm vegetables with unblemished skins. Buy them loose, if possible, rather than packed. Keep them in the refrigerator for up to a week, except avocados, which should be chilled for a maximum of two days.

Mushrooms & The Onion Family

Garlic Leeks Cultivated and wild mushrooms Onions

Cooks would be lost without these essential ingredients—the many varieties of onions and mushrooms flavor and add aroma and bulk to everything from delicately flavored cooking stocks to filling baked casseroles. Although garlic and onions have a pungent, full flavor, slow, gentle cooking transforms them to sweet richness. Red onions and scallions can also be eaten raw.

Cultivated mushrooms are often bland, more valued for their texture than their flavor, but experiment with different wild mushrooms and enjoy their intense flavors when cooked or added raw to salads.

Only buy onions and heads of garlic that feel heavy for their size with dry, papery skins; avoid any sprouting ones. Leeks should be firm with white bottoms and "fresh" green tops. Scallions should also be firm, not limp. Scallions are best kept in the refrigerator, but leeks will last for up to a week in a cool, dry place.

Brassicas & Leaves

Arugula Bok Choy Broccoli Brussels sprouts Cabbage Cauliflower Chicory Lettuce Spinach Watercress

These fresh green vegetables are equally tempting raw in salads or cooked, with arugula and watercress adding a zingy, peppery note. Broccoli, Brussels sprouts, cabbage, and cauliflower are members of the vitamin C-rich brassica family, and contain compounds that are believed to reduce the risk of cancer.

For maximum nutritional value, buy whole heads, rather than broccoli and cauliflower florets, avoiding any brown leaves. Brussels sprouts should have firm, tight leaves, and bok choy should have crisp, not limp, leaves. Look for fresh arugula, spinach, and watercress leaves without any wilting, store in the refrigerator, and use within two days of purchase. Mixed salad greens can be bought in sealed bags, conveniently washed and ready for use, but the washing process often depletes the nutrients. If you grow your own salad greens, try to pick them early in the morning, for same-day use, and store them in a plastic bag in the refrigerator.

TYPES OF FRUITS

Like vegetables, the range of fruits from which to choose is incredibly diverse. It is easy to get into a routine of buying the same types every week, but it really is worth experimenting with new varieties and broadening your culinary repertoire.

The ultimate convenience food, most fruits simply need a wash and are ready to eat. Since most nutrients are found just below the skin, avoid peeling if possible and preferably eat them raw instead of cooked, because the cooking process depletes nutrient levels. Good quality and freshness are essential when buying fruits; not only will they taste better and last longer, but they will be higher in antioxidant nutrients. Buy organic whenever you can and avoid buying in bulk if the fruits will be sitting in a fruit bowl or the refrigerator for days.

Citrus fruit
Vibrantly colored oranges, lemons, grapefruit, clementines, and limes are packed with beneficial vitamin C and beta carotene. They make a versatile addition to the kitchen, lending themselves to both sweet and

savory dishes. Once cut or peeled, use straight away, because vitamin C levels diminish from the moment the fruit is cut or sliced.

Orange
Popular varieties of orange include the juicy Jaffa, Valencia, and navel (named after the belly button-type spot at the flower end.) Thin-skinned oranges tend to be the juiciest. Marmalade is made from the sour-tasting Seville orange. Orange zest or peel adds a fragrant note to cakes, cookies, sweet sauces, and desserts, as well as savory dishes.

Lemon
Lemons (juice and zest) are an essential ingredient in the kitchen; just a squeeze of juice will add zing to salad dressings, vegetables, and marinades. The zest also enlivens both sweet and savory dishes. Lemon juice can also prevent some fruits and vegetables, such as avocado and apples, from

discoloring when cut. Avoid those with green patches on the skin, because this is a sign of unripeness.

Lime
Limes have a sharper flavor than lemons and are often used in Indian, Indonesian, and Thai cooking, adding a fragrant note.

How to Segment Citrus Fruit

Use a serrated knife to cut off a slice from the top and bottom of the fruit to reveal the flesh. Remove the skin and white pith, either in a spiral, beginning at the cut top and following the curve of the fruits, or by standing the fruit on the cut bottom and cutting down from top to bottom around the fruit.

Hold the fruit in the palm of your hand over a bowl. Use a small fruit knife to cut in front of the membrane. Push the knife forward to remove the segment cleanly from the membrane. Cut in front of the next membrane, then again push the knife forward toward the outer edge of the fruit—the segment will drop into the bowl.

Continue to separate all the segments from the membrane, then squeeze the membrane tightly. Unless using the segments immediately, put them in a small bowl, cover with plastic wrap, and refrigerate to prevent the air from oxidizing the fruit and making it bitter.

Orchard fruit
Probably the most popular group of fruits, ranging from crisp apples to succulent peaches and juicy cherries.

Apple
There are hundreds of different varieties of apple, and many stores are now beginning to stock some of the more unusual types. The Granny Smith is a good choice for a cooking apple, but does require sweetening with sugar. Some apples for eating raw are equally good stewed in a little water and no extra sugar is required.

Peach/Nectarine
Gorgeous succulent peaches range in color from gold to deep red and the flesh can be golden or white. Nectarines are similar, but without the fuzzy skin. Buy both peaches and nectarines slightly hard and then ripen them at home. They bruise easily, so be careful when handling them.

Pear
Like certain apples, some varieties of pear are good for cooking, while others are best eaten raw. Pears are best in the late summer and fall with the arrival of the new season's crop. Particular favorites are the plump Comice, the russett-yellow Bosc, and the yellow-skinned Bartletts.

Cherry
Glossy, sweet, red cherries make a welcome appearance in stores in the summer months. There are two types of cherry: sweet and sour. The latter is best when cooked.

Plum
Plums are a popular summer fruit and vary in color and flavor from yellow to purple and from the sweet and juicy to the slightly tart. The latter are best cooked in pies and cakes.

Currants
These glossy beads of brightly colored fruit make a pretty addition to desserts. Black currants, white currants, and red currants are usually sold in bunches on the stem. To remove the currants from the stalk, run the tines of a fork down through the clusters, being careful not to damage the fruit. Currants can be a little on the tart side and may benefit from a sprinkling of sugar. They look attractive in fruit salads, pies, and many delicious desserts, or they can easily be transformed into jellies and preserves.

Berries

Usually at their best in the summer, most berries are now readily available all year round.

Strawberry

Strawberries, if at their peak of ripeness (avoid those with white or green tips), need little embellishment; a spoonful of cream or yogurt will suffice. Strawberries contain plenty of vitamin C, and they are a good source of B vitamins.

Raspberry

Raspberries are very fragile and don't have a long shelf life. Their soft, delicate texture and aromatic flavor are best suited to simple preparations.

Gooseberry

Gooseberries are popular in northern Europe, but relatively rare in other parts of the world. They range from the tart green variety with the fuzzy skin, which is best suited to pies, other baked desserts, and jellies, to the softer, sweeter, purple type. The sweeter type can be mixed with cream or custard to make a fruit fool.

Blackberry

Blackberries can be seen in hedges in early fall, but the cultivated type have a longer season. Juicy and plump, blackberries vary in sweetness. Often used in cooking, they are delicious in tarts, pies, and other baked desserts, or pureed to make a sauce that goes with ice cream or nut roasts.

Blueberry

Ripe blueberries are plump and slightly firm, with a natural "bloom." They are delicious eaten raw, but can also be made into jellies and preserves, and baked into pies, tarts, cakes, and muffins.

Grapes

Grapes range in color from deep purple to pale red, and from vibrant green to almost white. Most grapes are grown for wine production; those for eating tend to be less acidic and have a thinner skin. Try to buy organic grapes or wash well before eating. The fruit should be plump and firm, and firmly attached to the stalk.

Melons

When buying melons, look for those that are heavy for their size, yield to gentle pressure, and smell fragrant at the stem end—this is a sign of

ripeness. There is a wide range, including the pinkish-red watermelon, yellow honeydew, and orange-fleshed cantaloupe. Watermelons are very low in calories owing to their high-water content and make a refreshing summer dessert. Avoid buying them already sliced because vitamin levels will have diminished.

Tropical fruit

This exotic collection of fruit ranges from the popular banana to the more unusual papaya.

Banana

The high starch content of bananas means they provide plenty of energy as well as fiber, vitamins, and minerals. The soft, creamy flesh can be baked whole, frozen to make a quick ice cream, blended into smoothies, or mashed into cakes. Bananas with green patches can be ripened at room temperature, but do not buy entirely green bananas because they rarely ripen properly.

Pineapple

Pineapples have a sweet and juicy flesh. Choose fruit that is heavy for its size and is slightly tender when pressed, with fresh green spiky leaves. The fruit is ripe when you can successfully pull out a leaf without tugging. Pineapples are particularly good for the digestive system.

Papaya

The slightly pear-shaped papaya has a speckled yellow skin when ripe, a vibrant pinkish-orange pulp, and an incredibly perfumed flavor. The numerous edible seeds taste peppery when dried. Papaya is best eaten raw, although unripe green fruit can be used in cooking.

Mango

Mangoes have a marvelously fragrant, juicy pulp when ripe, which can be used in a wide range of both sweet and savory dishes, turned into smoothies, ice cream, purees, and sauces, and added to salsas and salads. The skin ranges in color from green to yellow, orange, or red. A mango that is entirely green is likely to be unripe, although in Asia these are often sliced into salads.

Kiwi

Kiwis, or Chinese gooseberries, are particularly rich in vitamin C. The pureed flesh can be used to make refreshing sorbets and ice creams. Slice them in half and scoop out the flesh and seeds with a spoon for a healthy snack, or use in fruit salads.

Passion fruit

Passion fruit does not look particularly inviting, with its dark, wrinkly skin, but inside is a fragrant mixture of golden pulp and edible black seeds.

TYPES OF GRAINS, CEREALS, & BEANS

When we think of grains, rice, wheat, and oats immediately spring to mind, yet this group is surprisingly large and each type comes in various forms, from the whole grain to flour. For most of us, grains form a major part of our diet, and a very nutritious one at that. They are not only high in complex carbohydrates, they also contain essential protein, fiber, vitamins, and minerals, and are low in fat. Unprocessed types, such as those used in whole wheat bread and pasta, are richer in these nutrients because the refining process depletes much of the goodness of the grain. Inexpensive and readily available, grains make a versatile addition to the pantry.

To ensure freshness, always buy grains and their related products from stores that have a regular turnover of stock. Store in airtight containers in a cool, dry, dark cupboard to prevent them from becoming stale and to keep moisture out.

Wheat
The most widely available grain crop in the Western world, wheat comes in various forms.

Storing and Reusing Cooked Rice

Leftover cooked rice can be kept in an airtight container in the refrigerator. Make sure it is thoroughly cooled before refrigerating. If it is being used cold in salads, chill and use within a day. Reheat cooked rice thoroughly. Microwave it until it is piping hot or tip it into a saucepan of boiling water and reheat it for only 1 minute, or steam it over boiling water. If it is not used within two days, cooked rice is susceptible to a bacteria, *Bacillus cereus*, which can cause stomach upsets. Do not leave cooked rice uncovered at room temperature.

Flour

Flour is ground from the whole grain and may be whole wheat or white, depending on the degree of processing. Strong or hard flour is high in gluten, which makes it ideal for breadmaking, while soft flour is lower in gluten and higher in starch, making it better for cakes and pie dough. Durum wheat flour is one of the hardest wheat varieties and is used to make pasta.

Other forms of wheat

Wheat comes in many forms, including wheat berries, bran flakes, cracked wheat, bulgur wheat, wheat grass, couscous, and semolina. The latter, which looks like a grain, is actually a form of pasta made by steaming and drying cracked durum wheat.

Rice

Almost every culture in the world has its own culinary repertoire of rice dishes, ranging from Spanish paella to Indian biryani.

Long-grain and brown rice

Long-grain rice is the most widely used type of rice; brown rice has a nuttier, chewier texture than white, which contains less fiber and fewer nutrients.

Basmati

Basmati, available in both white and brown varieties, is a slender, long-grain rice and is aged for a year after harvest. Widely used in Indian dishes, its light, fluffy grain is also good for rice salads.

Thai and Japanese rice

Thai or jasmine rice has a soft, sticky texture and a mild, perfumed flavor, which explains its other name, fragrant rice. Japanese rice also has a soft, sticky texture and is mixed with rice vinegar to make sushi rolls.

Arborio, Carnaroli, and Valencia

Arborio and Carnaroli are classic risotto rices. The short, stubby grain absorbs about five times its weight in water, creating a creamy result. Valencia rice, used for paella, is also a short-grain rice, but it is not quite as starchy as risotto rice.

Other forms of rice

Other forms to look out for are pudding rice, red rice, and wild rice; the latter, with its slender black grains, is not in fact a true rice but an aquatic grass.

Other grains

Oats

Like rye, oats are a popular grain in Northern Europe. Rolled, or old-fashioned, oats are used to make porridge and muesli. Medium and fine oatmeal is best in oatcakes and breads. Oats are believed to reduce cholesterol levels in the blood.

Corn

Corn is also known as maize, and it comes in yellow, blue, red, and even black varieties. We are usually most familiar with yellow corn, which is used for cornmeal, cornstarch, and popcorn.

Rye

Rye flour is commonly used to make a dark, dense bread, particularly in Eastern Europe, Scandinavia, and Russia. The strong-tasting grain can also be used in savory dishes.

Quinoa

This highly nutritious grain is one of the few plant foods that is a complete protein, which means it contains all eight essential amino acids. The tiny beadlike grain has a mild, slightly bitter taste and can be used to make tabbouleh, stuffings, bakes, pilafs, and breakfast cereals.

Millet

This grain is not widely used, but it is highly nutritious, containing more iron than most other grains, and is a good source of zinc. The tiny beadlike grains have a mild flavor and make the perfect accompaniment to stews and curries, and can be used in pilafs, tabbouleh, milk desserts, and porridge. Millet is also gluten-free.

Barley

Pearl barley is the most common form and is husked, steamed, and polished to give it its characteristic ivory-colored look. Pot barley is the whole grain and takes much longer to cook than pearl. Both types make a satisfying porridge and can be added to stews, bakes, and soups.

HERBS & SPICES

Highly regarded for thousands of years, herbs and spices can enliven even the simplest of dishes. Invaluable ingredients in the vegetarian kitchen, they enhance the aroma and flavor of both savory and sweet dishes. They also have a positive effect on the digestive system. Although the directory of herbs below concentrates on fresh herbs, dried herbs provide a useful alternative, especially during the winter months when some fresh herbs are not going to be available.

Herbs

Fresh herbs are now sold loose, in pots or packages. It is possible to increase the shelf life of the latter by removing the herbs from the package and immersing the stems in a jar of water. Cover with a plastic bag, then seal with a rubber band; the herbs should keep for up to a week.

Basil

Basil is a popular fresh herb and is commonly used in Italian dishes, especially pesto. The purple variety is widely used in Thai cooking. The fragile leaves are best torn instead of cut with a knife to prevent them from bruising. Drying basil impairs its taste and so is not recommended.

Cilantro

A favorite in Thai cooking, the distinctive flavor of cilantro also enlivens Indian and Greek dishes. The root is edible and can be ground into Indian and Thai curry pastes.

Mint

There are numerous varieties of mint, with peppermint and spearmint being the most readily available. Mint can be mixed with plain yogurt to make raita, a calming accompaniment to hot curries; immersed in hot water to make a refreshing mint tea; or used in the fragrant salad, tabbouleh.

Dill

Dill is a scented herb. The featherlike leaves of the plant are used as a herb, while the seeds come from the flower heads after they have matured.

Tarragon

Tarragon is popular in French cooking and has a great affinity for egg and cheese dishes.

Chives

Chives are a part of the onion family, but have a milder flavor that works best when sprinkled over salads, eggs, and tomato-based dishes as a garnish.

Bay

The attractive, glossy, green leaves of the bay tree add a robust, spicy flavor to stocks and stews, and are used in bouquet garni. The leaf is used whole and is usually removed before the end of cooking because it is not readily digestible.

Oregano

Oregano is one of the few fresh herbs that dry well. Closely related to marjoram, but with a more robust flavor, oregano particularly complements tomato-based dishes. Both oregano and thyme work well in marinades and are largely interchangeable in their uses.

Parsley

Both flat-leaf and curly parsley are commonly available. Flat-leaf parsley looks similar to cilantro and is preferable to the curly type for use in cooking.

Sage, rosemary, and thyme

Sage is pungent in flavor, but works well with nut roasts, bakes, and stews. Rosemary has a strong, aromatic flavor and works best in hearty soups and stews where the flavors will not be overwhelmed. Thyme has a strong piquant or lemony flavor.

Spices

Spices—the seeds, fruits, pods, bark, and buds of plants—should be bought in small quantities from a store with a regular turnover of stock. Aroma is the best indication of freshness, since this diminishes when a spice is stale. Store spices in airtight jars away from direct sunlight.

Ginger
Ginger has a warming, slightly peppery flavor that is different from the fresh root. It is used to flavor cakes, breads, and cookies, and is added to curries, stews, and soups.

Cardamom
Pungent, warm, and aromatic, the spice known as cardamom is derived from several plants. It is sold as a seed pod or ground as a spice.

Cumin and coriander
A key component in Middle Eastern, North African, and Indian cooking, cumin is available ground and in whole seed form. Black seeds, also known as nigella, have a sweeter and milder flavor than the brown seeds. Ground coriander is used in much the same way as cumin, while the ivory-colored whole seeds are often used as a pickling spice as well as ground in curries and tagines.

Cinnamon, nutmeg, and cloves
These have a marvelously warming flavor and are often used together in cakes, desserts, and cookies. Whole cinnamon sticks (quills) are used to flavor curries, pilafs, and fruit compotes.

Saffron
Saffron is the world's most expensive spice. Made from the dried stigmas of *Crocus sativus*, only a tiny amount is required to add a distinctive flavor and a golden color to paella, stews, and milky desserts.

Pepper
Pepper is undoubtedly the most widely used spice and comes in a multitude of colors—black, white, pink, and green. The spice adds its own flavor to dishes and brings out the flavor of other ingredients.

Cayenne and paprika
Cayenne is a fiery spice that adds color and flavor to curries, soups, and stews. Paprika is milder and can be

used more liberally. Both are said to be good for the circulation.

Vanilla
Vanilla beans provide a fragrant, mellow, sweet taste, with a rich, perfumed aroma. They are often used in sweet dishes.

How to Freeze Herbs

Herbs must be in perfect condition before they are frozen. Anything stale, bruised, or contaminated will not be improved by freezing.

Wash the herbs carefully and shake dry. Lay out on paper towels to dry completely, transfer to a tray, and open freeze in a single layer. Once frozen, pack into small bags or boxes and use as required. Alternatively, chop the washed and dried herbs (they will bruise and blacken if they are not dry) and pack into ice-cube trays until half filled. Top up with water and freeze. Drop the herb ice cubes into stews, soups, and casseroles for an instant herb seasoning.

ESSENTIAL COOKING TECHNIQUES

While most vegetables can be eaten raw, there are numerous cooking techniques that will add interest and variety to vegetarian meals. You can maximize the flavor, color, and texture of the vegetables, while preserving as many of the essential vitamins and nutrients as possible. Since vegetables are so central to the vegetarian diet, it's well worth considering how best to cook them.

Boiling

The traditional method of cooking vegetables is to use plenty of salted water and a large, uncovered saucepan. This method is most suitable for corn, and for potatoes and other root vegetables. Although steaming is preferable when cooking green vegetables because they retain more nutrients, if you choose to boil them, leave them uncovered because putting the lid on makes them lose their attractive bright green color. Choose an appropriate size of saucepan for the quantity of vegetables so that the water can circulate, but use the minimum amount of water, cook for the briefest period, and drain the vegetables immediately, because boiling destroys water-soluble vitamins, such as B and C. Other soluble nutrients leach into the cooking water, so get into the habit of keeping the cooking water and using it as a basis for soups or sauces.

Freshly Prepared...

The fresher the ingredients, the higher their nutrient content. Avoid old, tired, wilted vegetables and do not store anything for long at home. It is far better to buy fresh and loose when you need them, and to select organic ingredients if you can, in preference to prepared packages, which will have lost some of their vitamins as well as their flavor. If possible, avoid peeling vegetables, because many nutrients are stored close to or in the skin (or put the peels into a pot to make stock.) Wash or scrub everything, but don't let vegetables soak in water or their soluble nutrients will leach out. Similarly, do not cut or prepare vegetables too far in advance, because some vitamins, such as vitamin C, diminish once the cut surface is exposed to the air.

Poaching

A less vigorous way to cook more delicate vegetables is to put them in boiling liquid (water, stock, wine, or milk), then to simmer them gently over low heat to retain their flavor, texture, and shape.

Frying

Deep-frying is less popular these days, with concerns over the amount of fat in our diet. However, if the cooking temperature is high enough, deep-fried foods are quickly sealed and absorb less oil than when they are shallow-fried. Coating vegetables in batter or in egg and breadcrumbs forms a crispy seal, which also reduces oil absorption. Deep-frying is a long-established cooking method for French fries and also works well for eggplants and zucchini. Dry-frying in a skillet or griddle pan or on a flat griddle plate is a healthier option that can be used for some vegetables as well as for halloumi cheese.

Steaming

Less water comes into contact with vegetables when they are steamed rather than boiled, so they are crisper and retain more essential nutrients. Also, some vegetables—snow peas, leeks, and zucchini—become limp and unappetizing if boiled. Steamed new potatoes are particularly delicious; try putting some fresh mint leaves under the potatoes to flavor them while they are steaming.

Braising

This cooking method requires only a very little water, and the saucepan is covered. The heat is much reduced and the cooking time greatly increased. You can start by browning the ingredients in a little oil or butter,

Cooking Times

For maximum nutritional benefit, it makes sense to cook your vegetables for the least time possible. Cut them to the same size so that they look attractive and cook evenly. While potatoes have to be cooked all the way through, other root vegetables, such as carrots, are best served with a little "bite" to them. Boil for less time or steam your vegetables and enjoy the extra crunch. Some vegetables—those with a high-water content, such as spinach, celery, or bean sprouts—need only be blanched in boiling water for 30 seconds. For frying or stir-frying, ensure that the oil is sufficiently hot before adding the vegetables. When time is short, try microwaving your vegetables. This method requires less liquid or fat as well as shorter cooking times than conventional cooking.

then add water or other liquid before covering the saucepan. The small amount of liquid that remains at the end of cooking will be sweet and flavored—serve the vegetables with this juice and you gain all the nutrients. Onions, turnips, leeks, chicory, celery, and fennel lend themselves to braising. Red cabbage is one of the brassicas that positively benefits from this long, slow method of cooking.

Stir-frying

This method of cooking in a little oil over very high heat has become widely popular. Stir-fried vegetables retain far more of their nutritional value, flavor, texture, and color. They are very thinly sliced and rapidly moved around in a hot wok to aid fast and even cooking. Most of us are familiar with stir-fried baby corn, snow peas, bell peppers, bean sprouts, and bamboo shoots, but the method is an equally good way to cook thinly sliced cauliflower, Brussels sprouts, cabbage, and carrots.

Roasting

Traditionally, roasting vegetables meant cooking them in the fat dripping from a joint of meat. The far healthier vegetarian option is to roast vegetables that have been lightly drizzled with olive oil in a roasting pan, to which you can add garlic and herbs for additional flavor. Squashes, parsnips, potatoes, bell peppers, onions, tomatoes, asparagus, and even beets are all delicious cooked in this way; their flavor is concentrated and the natural sweetness of the vegetables is accentuated.

Sauteing and sweating

These methods use less oil than traditional shallow-frying and are longer, slower processes than stir-frying. Sauteing is done in an uncovered skillet; sweating is done in either a heavy-bottom lidded casserole or skillet—water evaporating from the ingredients is trapped and falls back into the pan. Onions are often sweated to soften them without coloring.

Baking

Potatoes, onions, and garlic can be baked "dry" in their skins, while softer vegetables (bell peppers and tomatoes) can be stuffed with rice and other fillings or wrapped in foil.

Broiling and barbecuing

The intense heat from a broiler or barbecue is unsuitable for either delicate or dense vegetables, which become charred rather than cooked, but excellent for softer ones, such as onions, corn, bell peppers, eggplants, and tomatoes. All vegetables need to be brushed with oil before being placed under the broiler or on a barbecue grill.

BASIC RECIPES

The recipes in this book provide a wide variety of delicious vegetarian meals. Some of them incorporate a common basic recipe, to which you can refer on these pages, or you can use these basic recipes as an addition to a dish of your choice.

VEGETABLE STOCK
MAKES: 4½ PINTS/2 LITERS

- 2 TBSP SUNFLOWER OIL OR CORN OIL
- I MEDIUM ONION, FINELY CHOPPED
- ½ CUP FINELY CHOPPED LEEKS
- ¾ CUP FINELY CHOPPED CARROTS
- 4 CELERY STALKS, FINELY CHOPPED
- 3 OZ/85 G FENNEL, FINELY CHOPPED
- 1 SMALL TOMATO, FINELY CHOPPED
- 4¾ PINTS/2.25 LITERS WATER
- 1 BOUQUET GARNI

Heat the oil in a large saucepan over low heat. Add the onions and leeks and cook, stirring frequently, for 5 minutes, or until soft.

Add the remaining vegetables, cover, and cook over very low heat, stirring occasionally, for 10 minutes. Add the water and bouquet garni and bring to a boil, then reduce the heat and simmer for 20 minutes.

Strain, cool, then cover and store in the refrigerator. Use within 3 days or freeze in portions for up to 3 months.

CHEESE SAUCE
MAKES: 2½ CUPS

- 3 TBSP BUTTER
- 5 TBSP ALL-PURPOSE FLOUR
- 2½ CUPS MILK
- 1¼ CUPS CHEDDAR CHEESE, GRATED
- SALT AND PEPPER

Melt the butter in a saucepan over medium heat. Stir in the flour and cook, stirring constantly, for 1–2 minutes.

Remove from the heat and gradually whisk in the milk. Return to the heat and bring to a boil, whisking constantly. Simmer for 2 minutes, or until the sauce is thick and glossy. Remove from the heat, add the cheese, and stir until melted. Season to taste with salt and pepper.

TOMATO SAUCE
MAKES: ⅔ CUP

- 1 TBSP OLIVE OIL
- 1 SMALL ONION, CHOPPED
- 1 GARLIC CLOVE, CHOPPED
- 14 OZ/400 G CANNED CHOPPED TOMATOES
- 2 TBSP CHOPPED FRESH PARSLEY
- 1 TSP DRIED OREGANO
- 2 BAY LEAVES
- 2 TBSP TOMATO PASTE
- 1 TSP SUGAR
- SALT AND PEPPER

Heat the oil in a saucepan over medium heat. Add the onion and cook, stirring, for 2–3 minutes, until beginning to soften.

Add the garlic and cook, stirring, for 1 minute. Stir in the tomatoes, parsley, oregano, bay leaves, tomato paste, and sugar, and season to taste with salt and pepper. Bring the sauce to a boil, then reduce the heat and simmer, uncovered, for 15–20 minutes, until the sauce has reduced by half. Remove and discard the bay leaves just before serving.

PESTO SAUCE
MAKES: ⅓ CUP

- 3 CUPS FRESH BASIL LEAVES
- ½ OZ/15 G PINE NUTS
- 1 GARLIC CLOVE
- PINCH OF SALT
- ¼ CUP FRESHLY GRATED PARMESAN CHEESE
- 3 TBSP EXTRA VIRGIN OLIVE OIL

Put the basil leaves, pine nuts, garlic, and salt in a mortar, and pound to a paste with a pestle.

Transfer to a bowl and, with a wooden spoon, gradually work in the Parmesan cheese, followed by the oil, to make a thick, creamy sauce.

Cover with plastic wrap and refrigerate until required.

MAYONNAISE
MAKES: 1¼ CUPS

- 2 EGG YOLKS
- ⅔ CUP SUNFLOWER OIL
- ⅔ CUP OLIVE OIL
- 1 TBSP WHITE WINE VINEGAR
- 2 TSP DIJON MUSTARD
- SALT AND PEPPER

Beat the egg yolks with a pinch of salt in a bowl. Whisk the oils together in a pitcher. Gradually add one-quarter of the oil mixture to the egg yolks, a drop at a time, beating constantly with a whisk or electric mixer. Beat in the vinegar, then continue adding the oils in a steady stream, beating constantly.

Once all the oil has been incorporated, stir in the mustard, and season to taste with salt and pepper.

TZATZIKI

MAKES: 2¼ CUPS

- 2¼ CUPS PLAIN GREEK-STYLE YOGURT OR OTHER THICK PLAIN YOGURT
- 4 GARLIC CLOVES, VERY FINELY CHOPPED
- 2 CUCUMBERS, PEELED, SEEDED, AND VERY FINELY DICED
- 1 TBSP LEMON-FLAVORED OIL OR EXTRA VIRGIN OLIVE OIL
- 3 TBSP LEMON JUICE
- 1 TBSP CHOPPED FRESH MINT LEAVES
- SALT AND PEPPER
- PAPRIKA, TO GARNISH

TO SERVE
- CELERY BATONS
- CARROT BATONS
- PITA TRIANGLES

Put the yogurt, garlic, cucumbers, oil, lemon juice, and mint in a serving bowl and stir together until well combined. Season to taste with salt and pepper, cover with plastic wrap, and chill in the refrigerator for at least 2 hours, or until required.

When ready to use, garnish with a little paprika. Serve with the celery and carrot batons and the pita triangles for dipping.

RICH FLAKY PIE DOUGH

MAKES: ONE 9-INCH/23-CM TART

- 1¼ CUPS ALL-PURPOSE FLOUR
- PINCH OF SALT
- 6 TBSP BUTTER, DICED, PLUS EXTRA FOR GREASING
- 1 EGG YOLK
- 3 TBSP ICE-COLD WATER

Sift the flour with the salt into a bowl. Add the butter and rub into the flour with your fingertips until the mixture resembles fine breadcrumbs.

Beat the egg yolk with the water in a small bowl. Sprinkle the liquid over the flour mixture and combine with a round-bladed knife or your fingertips to form a dough. Shape the dough into a ball, wrap in foil, and chill in the refrigerator for 30 minutes.

PUFF PIE DOUGH
MAKES: ONE 10-INCH/25-CM TART OR PIE

- 1¼ CUPS ALL-PURPOSE FLOUR, PLUS EXTRA FOR DUSTING
- PINCH OF SALT
- ¾ CUP UNSALTED BUTTER
- ABOUT ⅔ CUP ICE-COLD WATER

Sift the flour with the salt into a large bowl. Dice 2 tablespoons of the butter and rub into the flour with your fingertips. Gradually add the water, just enough to bring the mixture together, and knead briefly to form a smooth dough. Wrap the dough in foil and chill in the refrigerator for 30 minutes.

Keep the remaining butter out of the refrigerator, wrap in foil, and shape into a 1¼-inch/3-cm thick rectangle. Roll out the dough on a lightly floured counter to a rectangle 3 times longer and 1¼ inches/3 cm wider than the butter. Unwrap the butter and place in the center of the dough, long side toward you. Fold over the 2 "wings" of dough to enclose the butter, press down the edges with the rolling pin to seal, and then turn the dough so that the short side is facing you. Roll out the dough to its original length, fold in 3, turn and roll again to its original length.

Repeat this once more, then rewrap the dough and chill again for 30 minutes. Repeat the rolling and turning twice more. Chill again for 30 minutes. At this point you can freeze the dough until you need it.

PIZZA DOUGH
MAKES: TWO 10-INCH/25-CM PIZZAS

- GENEROUS 1½ CUPS ALL-PURPOSE FLOUR, PLUS EXTRA FOR DUSTING
- 1 TSP SALT
- 6 TBSP LUKE-WARM WATER
- 2 TBSP OLIVE OIL, PLUS EXTRA FOR OILING
- 1 TSP ACTIVE DRY YEAST

Sift the flour with the salt into a large, warmed bowl and make a well in the center. Add the water, oil, and yeast to the well. Using a wooden spoon or your hands, gradually mix in, drawing the flour from the sides, to form a dough.

Turn out on to a lightly floured counter and knead for 5 minutes, or until smooth and elastic. Form the dough into a ball, put in a clean, lightly oiled bowl, and cover with oiled plastic wrap. Let stand in a warm place to rise for 1 hour, or until doubled in size.

Turn out the dough onto a lightly floured counter and knock back. Knead briefly before shaping into 2 circles measuring 10 inches/25 cm in diameter.

1

SHOOTS, ROOTS
& STEMS

This chapter will give you new ideas for preparing some of the most familiar, everyday vegetables—Baked Celery with Cream, for example, will stop you from ever again thinking of celery as simply a low-calorie salad ingredient. Even the humble potato can take center stage in many recipes such as Roasted Potato Wedges with Shallots & Rosemary, and Caramelized Sweet Potatoes. And, for something lighter, try the stir-fried and bean sprout salad ideas.

SWEET POTATO & APPLE SOUP

SERVES 6

INGREDIENTS
- 1 TBSP BUTTER
- 3 LEEKS, THINLY SLICED
- 1 LARGE CARROT, THINLY SLICED
- 1¼ LB/550 G SWEET POTATOES, PEELED AND CUBED
- 2 LARGE TART APPLES, PEELED AND CUBED
- 5 CUPS WATER
- FRESHLY GRATED NUTMEG
- 1 CUP APPLE JUICE
- 1 CUP WHIPPING OR LIGHT CREAM
- SALT AND PEPPER
- SNIPPED FRESH CHIVES OR CILANTRO, TO GARNISH

1 Melt the butter in a large saucepan over medium–low heat. Add the leeks, then cover and cook for 6–8 minutes, or until soft, stirring frequently.

2 Add the carrot, sweet potatoes, apples, and water to the saucepan and season lightly with salt, pepper, and nutmeg. Bring to a boil, then reduce the heat and simmer, covered, for about 20 minutes, stirring occasionally, until the vegetables are very tender.

3 Let the soup cool slightly, then transfer to a blender or food processor and puree until smooth, working in batches if necessary. (If using a food processor, strain off the cooking liquid and reserve. Puree the soup solids with enough cooking liquid to moisten them, then combine with the remaining liquid.)

4 Return the puree soup to the saucepan and stir in the apple juice. Place over low heat and simmer for about 10 minutes, until heated through.

5 Stir in the cream and continue simmering for about 5 minutes, stirring frequently, until heated through. Taste and adjust the seasoning, adding more salt, pepper, and nutmeg, if necessary. Ladle the soup into warm bowls, then garnish with chives or cilantro and serve.

BEET SALAD

SERVES 4–6

INGREDIENTS

- 2 LB/900 G RAW BEETS
- 4 TBSP EXTRA VIRGIN OLIVE OIL
- 1½ TBSP RED WINE VINEGAR
- 2 GARLIC CLOVES, FINELY CHOPPED
- 2 SCALLIONS, CHOPPED
- COARSE SEA SALT
- GARLIC SAUCE, TO SERVE (OPTIONAL)

1 Carefully remove the roots from the beets without cutting into the skin, then cut off all but 1 inch/2.5 cm of the stalks. Gently rub the beets under cold running water, without splitting the skins, to remove any dirt. Put the beets in a saucepan with enough water to cover and bring to a boil. Cover, reduce the heat slightly, and cook for 25–40 minutes, depending on the size, until the largest beet is tender when you pierce it with a long metal skewer or knife.

2 Meanwhile, put the oil, vinegar, garlic, scallions, and salt to taste in a jar with a screw-top lid and shake until emulsified. Set aside.

3 Drain the beets and rinse under cold running water until cool enough to handle, then peel away the skins. Thickly chop or slice the beets, then put in a bowl and pour over the dressing. Cover and chill in the refrigerator for at least 1 hour.

4 To serve, gently toss the salad and transfer to a serving platter. Serve with a bowl of Garlic Sauce on the side, if using.

POTATO FRITTERS WITH ONION & TOMATO RELISH

SERVES 8

INGREDIENTS

- ⅓ CUP ALL-PURPOSE WHOLE WHEAT FLOUR
- 1½ TSP GROUND CORIANDER
- ½ TSP CUMIN SEEDS
- ¼ TSP CHILI POWDER
- ½ TSP GROUND TURMERIC
- ¼ TSP SALT
- 1 EGG
- 3 TBSP MILK
- 12 OZ/350 G POTATOES, PEELED
- 1–2 GARLIC CLOVES, CRUSHED
- 4 SCALLIONS, CHOPPED
- ¼ CUP CORN KERNELS
- VEGETABLE OIL, FOR SHALLOW- FRYING

ONION & TOMATO RELISH

- 1 ONION, PEELED
- 8 OZ/225 G TOMATOES
- 2 TBSP CHOPPED FRESH CILANTRO
- 2 TBSP CHOPPED FRESH MINT
- 2 TBSP LEMON JUICE
- ½ TSP ROASTED CUMIN SEEDS
- ¼ TSP SALT
- PINCH OF CAYENNE PEPPER

1 First make the relish. Dice the onion and tomatoes and place in a bowl with the remaining ingredients. Mix together well and let the relish stand for at least 15 minutes before serving to let the flavors blend.

2 Place the flour in a bowl, stir in the spices and salt, and make a well in the center. Add the egg and milk and mix to form a fairly thick batter.

3 Coarsely grate the potatoes, place them in a sieve, and rinse well under cold running water. Drain and squeeze dry, then stir them into the batter with the garlic, scallions, and corn. Mix to combine thoroughly.

4 Heat about ¼ inch/5 mm of vegetable oil in a large skillet and add a few tablespoons of the mixture at a time, flattening each one to form a thin fritter. Cook over low heat, turning frequently, for 2–3 minutes, or until golden brown and cooked through.

5 Drain the fritters on absorbent paper towels and keep them hot while cooking the remaining mixture in the same way. Serve the potato fritters hot with the onion and tomato relish.

ARTICHOKE & PIMIENTO FLATBREAD

MAKES 12 SLICES

INGREDIENTS

- 4 TBSP SPANISH OLIVE OIL, PLUS EXTRA FOR OILING
- 2 LARGE ONIONS, THINLY SLICED
- 2 GARLIC CLOVES, FINELY CHOPPED
- 14 OZ/400 G CANNED ARTICHOKE HEARTS, DRAINED AND QUARTERED
- 11¼ OZ/320 G BOTTLED OR CANNED PIMIENTOS DEL PIQUILLO, DRAINED AND THINLY SLICED
- SCANT ¼ CUP PITTED BLACK SPANISH OLIVES (OPTIONAL)
- SALT AND PEPPER

BREAD DOUGH

- GENEROUS 2¾ CUPS WHITE BREAD FLOUR, PLUS EXTRA FOR DUSTING
- 1½ TSP ACTIVE DRY YEAST
- 1 TSP SALT
- ½ TSP SUPERFINE SUGAR
- ¾ CUP WARM WATER
- 3 TBSP SPANISH OLIVE OIL

1 To make the bread dough, put the flour, yeast, salt, and sugar in a large bowl and make a well in the center. Mix the water and oil together in a pitcher and pour into the well, then gradually mix in the flour from the side. Using your hands, mix together to form a soft dough that leaves the side of the bowl clean.

2 Turn out the dough onto a lightly floured counter and knead for 10 minutes, or until smooth and elastic and no longer sticky. Shape the dough into a ball and put in a clean bowl. Cover with a clean, damp dish towel and let the bowl stand in a warm place for 1 hour, or until the dough has risen and doubled in size.

3 Meanwhile, heat 3 tablespoons of the oil in a large skillet, then add the onions and cook over medium heat, stirring occasionally, for 10 minutes, or until golden brown. Add the garlic and cook, stirring, for 30 seconds, or until softened. Cool. When cool, stir in the artichoke hearts and pimientos del piquillo, then season to taste with salt and pepper.

4 Preheat the oven to 400°F/200°C. Oil a large cookie sheet. Turn out the risen dough onto a lightly floured counter and knead lightly for 2–3 minutes to knock out the air. Roll out the dough to a 12-inch/30-cm square and transfer to the prepared cookie sheet.

5 Brush the remaining oil over the dough and spread the artichoke and pimiento mixture on top. Sprinkle over the olives, if using. Bake in the preheated oven for 20–25 minutes, or until golden brown and crisp. Cut into 12 slices and serve the flatbread hot or warm.

CARROT & ORANGE STIR-FRY

SERVES 4

INGREDIENTS

- 2 TBSP SUNFLOWER OIL
- 2¼ CUPS GRATED CARROTS
- 8 OZ/225 G LEEKS, SHREDDED
- 2 ORANGES, PEELED AND SEGMENTED
- 2 TBSP KETCHUP
- 1 TBSP RAW BROWN SUGAR
- 2 TBSP LIGHT SOY SAUCE
- ½ CUP CHOPPED PEANUTS

1 Heat the sunflower oil in a large preheated wok.

2 Add the grated carrots and leeks to the wok and cook for 2–3 minutes, or until the vegetables have just softened.

3 Add the orange segments to the wok and heat through gently, ensuring that you do not break up the orange segments as you stir the mixture.

4 Mix the ketchup, brown sugar, and light soy sauce in a small bowl.

5 Add the ketchup-and-sugar mixture to the wok and cook for an additional 2 minutes.

6 Transfer the stir-fry to warm serving bowls and scatter with the chopped peanuts. Serve immediately.

GARLIC MASH POTATOES

SERVES 4

INGREDIENTS

- 2 LB/900 G STARCHY POTATOES, CUT INTO CHUNKS
- 8 GARLIC CLOVES, CRUSHED
- ⅔ CUP MILK
- 6 TBSP BUTTER
- PINCH OF FRESHLY GRATED NUTMEG
- SALT AND PEPPER

1 Put the potatoes into a large saucepan. Add enough water to cover and a pinch of salt. Bring to a boil and cook for 10 minutes. Add the garlic and cook for an additional 10–15 minutes, or until the potatoes are tender.

2 Drain the potatoes and garlic, reserving 3 tablespoons of the cooking liquid. Return the reserved cooking liquid to the saucepan, then add the milk and bring to simmering point. Add the butter, return the potatoes and garlic to the pan, and turn off the heat. Mash thoroughly with a potato masher.

3 Season the potato mixture to taste with nutmeg, salt, and pepper and beat thoroughly with a wooden spoon until light and fluffy. Serve immediately.

CARAMELIZED SWEET POTATOES

SERVES 4

INGREDIENTS

- 1 LB/450 G SWEET POTATOES
- ½ CUP BUTTER
- ¼ CUP BROWN SUGAR, MAPLE SYRUP, OR HONEY
- 2 TBSP ORANGE JUICE OR PINEAPPLE JUICE
- ½ CUP PINEAPPLE PIECES (OPTIONAL)
- PINCH GROUND CINNAMON, NUTMEG, OR PUMPKIN SPICE (OPTIONAL)

1 Wash the sweet potatoes, but do not peel. Boil them in a large saucepan of salted water until just tender, for about 30–45 minutes, depending on their size. Remove from the heat and drain well. Cool slightly, then peel.

2 Preheat the oven to 400°F/200°C. Thickly slice the sweet potatoes and arrange in a single overlapping layer in a greased ovenproof dish. Cut the butter into small cubes and dot them over the top.

3 Sprinkle with the brown sugar and the fruit juice. Add the pineapple and spices, if using.

4 Bake for 30–40 minutes, basting occasionally, until golden brown.

ROASTED ROOT VEGETABLES

SERVES 4–6

INGREDIENTS

- 3 PARSNIPS, CUT INTO
  2-INCH/5-CM CHUNKS
- 4 BABY TURNIPS, QUARTERED
- 3 CARROTS, CUT INTO
  2-INCH/5-CM CHUNKS
- 1 LB/450 G BUTTERNUT
  SQUASH, PEELED AND CUT
  INTO 2-INCH/5-CM CHUNKS
- 1 LB/450 G SWEET POTATOES,
  PEELED AND CUT INTO
  2-INCH/5-CM CHUNKS
- 2 GARLIC CLOVES, FINELY
  CHOPPED
- 2 TBSP CHOPPED FRESH
  ROSEMARY
- 2 TBSP CHOPPED FRESH THYME
- 2 TSP CHOPPED FRESH SAGE
- 3 TBSP OLIVE OIL
- SALT AND PEPPER
- 2 TBSP CHOPPED FRESH MIXED
  HERBS, SUCH AS PARSLEY,
  THYME, AND MINT,
  TO GARNISH

1 Preheat the oven to 425°F/220°C.

2 Arrange all the vegetables in a single layer in a large roasting pan. Sprinkle over the garlic and the herbs. Pour over the oil and season well with salt and pepper.

3 Toss all the ingredients together until they are well mixed and coated with the oil (you can let them marinate at this stage to let the flavors be absorbed).

4 Roast the vegetables at the top of the preheated oven for 50–60 minutes, until they are cooked and nicely browned. Turn the vegetables over halfway through the cooking time.

5 Serve with a good handful of fresh herbs sprinkled on top and a final seasoning of salt and pepper to taste.

BAKED CELERY
WITH CREAM

SERVES 4

INGREDIENTS

- 1 HEAD OF CELERY
- ½ TSP GROUND CUMIN
- ½ TSP GROUND CORIANDER
- 1 GARLIC CLOVE, CRUSHED
- 1 RED ONION, THINLY SLICED
- SCANT ½ CUP PECAN HALVES
- ⅔ CUP VEGETABLE STOCK
- ⅔ CUP LIGHT CREAM
- 1 CUP FRESH WHOLE WHEAT
  BREADCRUMBS
- ¼ CUP FRESHLY GRATED
  PARMESAN CHEESE
- SALT AND PEPPER
- CELERY LEAVES, TO GARNISH

1 Preheat the oven to 400°F/200°C. Trim the celery and cut into short sticks. Place the celery in an ovenproof dish with the ground cumin and coriander, garlic, red onion, and pecans.

2 Mix the stock and cream together in a pitcher and pour over the vegetables. Season to taste with salt and pepper. Mix the breadcrumbs and cheese together in a small bowl and sprinkle over the top to cover the vegetables.

3 Cook in the preheated oven for 40 minutes, or until the vegetables are tender and the top is crispy. Garnish with celery leaves and serve.

ASPARAGUS WITH SWEET TOMATO DRESSING

SERVES 4

INGREDIENTS

- 5 TBSP EXTRA VIRGIN OLIVE OIL, PLUS EXTRA FOR BRUSHING
- ½ CUP PINE NUTS
- 12 OZ/350 G TOMATOES, PEELED, SEEDED, AND CHOPPED
- 2 TBSP BALSAMIC VINEGAR
- 1 LB 2 OZ/500 G YOUNG ASPARAGUS SPEARS, TRIMMED
- ¼ CUP THINLY SHAVED PARMESAN CHEESE
- SALT AND PEPPER

1 Brush a broiler pan with oil and preheat. Dry-fry the pine nuts in a heavy skillet for 30–60 seconds, until golden. Tip into a bowl and set aside.

2 Combine the tomatoes, vinegar, and olive oil in a bowl, and season with salt and pepper. Set aside.

3 When the broiler pan is hot, add the asparagus spears and cook for 3–4 minutes, until tender. Carefully transfer to a serving dish. Spoon the dressing over them, sprinkle with the pine nuts and Parmesan shavings, and serve immediately.

ASPARAGUS & SUN-DRIED TOMATO RISOTTO

SERVES 4

INGREDIENTS

- 4 CUPS VEGETABLE STOCK
- 1 TBSP OLIVE OIL
- 3 TBSP BUTTER
- 1 SMALL ONION, FINELY CHOPPED
- 6 SUN-DRIED TOMATOES, THINLY SLICED
- SCANT 1½ CUPS RISOTTO RICE
- ⅔ CUP DRY WHITE WINE
- 8 OZ/225 G FRESH ASPARAGUS SPEARS, COOKED
- ¾ CUP FRESHLY GRATED PARMESAN OR GRANA PADANO CHEESE
- SALT AND PEPPER
- THINLY PARED LEMON ZEST, TO GARNISH

1 Bring the stock to a boil in a saucepan, then reduce the heat and keep simmering gently over low heat while you are cooking the risotto.

2 Heat the oil with 2 tablespoons of the butter in a deep pan over medium heat until the butter has melted.

3 Stir in the onion and sun-dried tomatoes, and cook, stirring occasionally, for 5 minutes until the onion is soft and starting to turn golden. Do not brown.

4 Reduce the heat, add the rice, and mix to coat in oil and butter. Cook, stirring constantly, for 2–3 minutes, or until the grains are translucent.

5 Add the wine and cook, stirring constantly, until it has reduced.

6 Gradually add the hot stock, a ladleful at a time. Stir constantly and add more liquid as the rice absorbs each addition.

Increase the heat to medium so that the liquid bubbles. Cook for 20 minutes, or until all the liquid is absorbed and the rice is creamy. Season to taste.

7 While the risotto is cooking, cut most of the asparagus into pieces about 1-inch/2.5-cm long. Keep several spears whole for garnishing the finished dish. Carefully fold the cut pieces of asparagus into the risotto for the last 5 minutes of cooking time.

8 Remove the risotto from the heat and add the remaining butter. Mix well, then stir in the Parmesan until it melts. Spoon the risotto onto individual warmed serving dishes and garnish with whole spears of asparagus. Sprinkle the lemon zest on top and serve.

BEAN SPROUT SALAD

SERVES 4

INGREDIENTS

- 4 CUPS BEAN SPROUTS
- 1 SMALL CUCUMBER
- 1 GREEN BELL PEPPER, SEEDED AND CUT INTO MATCHSTICKS
- 1 CARROT, CUT INTO MATCHSTICKS
- 2 TOMATOES, FINELY CHOPPED
- 1 CELERY STALK, CUT INTO MATCHSTICKS
- 1 GARLIC CLOVE, CRUSHED
- DASH OF CHILI SAUCE
- 2 TBSP LIGHT SOY SAUCE
- 1 TSP WINE VINEGAR
- 2 TSP SESAME OIL
- FRESH CHIVES, TO GARNISH

1 Blanch the bean sprouts in boiling water for 1 minute. Drain well, rinse under cold water, then drain again.

2 Cut the cucumber in half lengthwise. Scoop out the seeds with a teaspoon and discard. Cut the flesh into matchsticks with a sharp knife and mix with the bean sprouts, green bell pepper, carrot, tomatoes, and celery in a large glass bowl.

3 Mix together the crushed garlic, chili sauce, soy sauce, wine vinegar, and sesame oil in a small bowl.

4 Pour the dressing over the vegetables, tossing well to coat the salad thoroughly.

5 Spoon the salad onto 4 individual serving plates. Garnish with fresh chives and serve immediately.

STIR-FRIED BEAN SPROUTS

SERVES 4

INGREDIENTS
- 1 TBSP VEGETABLE OIL OR PEANUT OIL
- GENEROUS 1½ CUPS BEAN SPROUTS, TRIMMED
- 2 TBSP FINELY CHOPPED SCALLION
- ½ TSP SALT
- PINCH OF SUGAR

1 In a preheated wok or deep pan, heat the oil and stir-fry the bean sprouts with the scallion for about 1 minute. Add the salt and sugar and stir. Remove and serve immediately.

FENNEL RISOTTO WITH VODKA

SERVES 4–5

INGREDIENTS
- 2 LARGE FENNEL BULBS
- 2 TBSP VEGETABLE OIL
- 6 TBSP UNSALTED BUTTER
- 1 LARGE ONION, FINELY CHOPPED
- 1¾ CUPS RISOTTO OR CARNAROLI RICE
- ⅔ CUP VODKA (OR LEMON-FLAVORED VODKA, IF YOU CAN FIND IT)
- 5⅔ CUPS LIGHT VEGETABLE STOCK, SIMMERING
- ⅔ CUP FRESHLY GRATED PARMESAN CHEESE
- 5–6 TBSP LEMON JUICE
- SALT AND PEPPER

1 Trim the fennel, reserving the fronds for the garnish, if desired. Cut the bulbs in half lengthwise, then remove the V-shaped cores and chop the flesh coarsely. (If you like, add any of the fennel trimmings to the stock for extra flavor.)

2 Heat the oil and half the butter in a large, heavy saucepan over medium heat. Add the onion and fennel and cook for about 2 minutes, stirring frequently, until the vegetables are soft. Add the rice and cook for about 2 minutes, stirring frequently, until the rice is translucent and well coated with oil and butter.

3 Pour the vodka into the rice. It will bubble rapidly and evaporate almost immediately. Add a ladleful of the stock. Cook, stirring constantly, until the ladleful of liquid is absorbed.

4 Continue stirring in the stock, about half a ladleful at a time, letting each addition be completely absorbed by the rice before adding the next. This should take about 20–25 minutes. The finished risotto should have a creamy consistency and the rice should be just tender, but firm to the bite.

5 Stir in the remaining butter, grated Parmesan cheese, and lemon juice. Remove from the heat, cover, and let the risotto stand for 1 minute.

6 Garnish the risotto with a few of the reserved fennel fronds, and serve.

2

FRUITS &
SQUASHES

Take advantage of the wide selection of tomatoes, bell peppers, and squashes that are now commonplace in markets and supermarkets with these exciting recipes. Eggplants, butternut squashes, zucchini, bell peppers, pumpkins, and tomatoes come in a variety of colors and shapes, but they all stand up well to long, gentle cooking and respond well to spices, making them ideal for soups, pasta sauces, and curries. The smooth, creamy texture of avocados can be transformed into delicious dips and soups.

DIRECTORY OF FRUITS & SQUASHES

Tomatoes, eggplants, chiles, avocados, and bell peppers are all vegetables, but botanically they are classified as fruits, which distinguishes them from roots, shoots, and flowering vegetables. This group includes some of the most versatile vegetables, suitable for most cooking methods—many of them can also be eaten raw.

Fruit vegetables
This nutritious group adds plenty of color and flavor to a range of dishes.

Eggplant
Known in the Middle East as "poor man's caviar", eggplant gives substance and flavor to spicy stews and tomato-based bakes, and can be roasted, broiled, or pureed into garlicky dips.

Tomatoes
There are now so many varieties of tomato from which to choose, from the sweet, bite-size cherry to the large beefsteak. The egg-shape plum tomato makes rich sauces, while sun-dried tomatoes add a sweet richness to dips, sauces, soups, and stews.

Chiles
Chiles have a crucial role in many cuisines, including Mexican, Indian, and Thai. There are hundreds of different types, which range in potency from the mild and flavorful to the blisteringly hot.

Bell peppers
Red, yellow, and orange bell peppers are an excellent source of vitamin C; green and purple to a lesser extent. Green bell peppers are fully developed, but are not as ripe as their more colorful counterparts, which can make them relatively difficult to digest.

Avocados
Avocados are rich in vitamins C and E and are said to improve the condition of the skin and hair. Brush them with lemon juice or lime juice after cutting to prevent the flesh from discoloring.

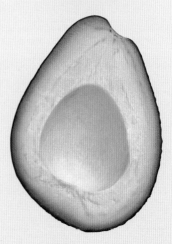

Avocados are usually served raw, but can also be baked.

Pumpkins and squashes

This group of vegetables comes in a wide range of colors, shapes, and sizes. They are broadly divided into two types: summer, which include cucumbers and zucchini, and winter, such as the various pumpkins and squashes.

Summer
Zucchini are at their best when small and young; the flavor diminishes and the seeds toughen as they grow older and larger. Extremely versatile, zucchini can be steamed, stir-fried, pureed, broiled, and roasted, as well as used in soups and casseroles. Their deep yellow flowers are perfect for stuffing. Look for firm, bright, unblemished vegetables that are heavy for their size.

Winter
Butternut squash is one of the most readily available winter types. A large, distinctively pear-shape vegetable with a golden skin and orange flesh, it is equally delicious mashed, baked, or roasted, or used in soups and stews, and makes a good substitute for pumpkin. Small pumpkins have a sweeter, less fibrous flesh than the large ones, which are probably best kept for making lanterns at Halloween!

How to Prepare Pumpkins and Squashes

These vegetables have thick skins, which are usually removed before cooking. Select a large, heavy knife and put a damp dish towel under the cutting board so that it doesn't slip. Cut off a slice from the bottom to make it flat, and cut off the stalk end, too. Stand the vegetable on the flat bottom and cut away the tough skin with firm, vertical slices for butternut squashes or follow the curve for round varieties and pumpkins. Slice in half and use a large spoon to scrape out all the seeds and fibers. Dice or slice the flesh.

AVOCADO & ALMOND SOUP

SERVES 4

INGREDIENTS

- 2½ CUPS WATER
- 1 ONION, FINELY CHOPPED
- 1 CELERY STALK, FINELY CHOPPED
- 1 CARROT, GRATED
- 4 GARLIC CLOVES, CHOPPED OR CRUSHED
- 1 BAY LEAF
- SCANT 1 CUP GROUND ALMONDS
- 2 RIPE AVOCADOS (ABOUT 1 LB/450 G)
- 3–4 TBSP FRESH LEMON JUICE
- SALT
- CHOPPED FRESH CHIVES, TO GARNISH

1 Combine the water, onion, celery, carrot, garlic, bay leaf, and ½ teaspoon salt in a saucepan. Bring to a boil, reduce the heat, cover, and simmer for about 30 minutes, or until the vegetables are very tender.

2 Strain the mixture, reserving the liquid and the vegetables separately. Remove and discard the bay leaf.

3 Put the vegetables into a blender or food processor. Add the almonds and a small amount of the liquid and process to a very smooth puree, scraping down the sides as necessary. Add as much of the remaining liquid as the capacity of the blender or processor permits and process to combine. Scrape into a bowl, stir in any remaining liquid, cover, and chill until cold.

4 Cut the avocados in half, discard the pits, and scoop the flesh into the blender or food processor. Add the cold soup and process to a smooth puree, scraping down the sides as necessary. For a thinner consistency, add a few spoonfuls of cold water.

5 Add the lemon juice and season with salt to taste. Ladle into chilled small bowls and sprinkle each serving lightly with chopped chives.

GUACAMOLE

SERVES 4

INGREDIENTS

- 1 RIPE TOMATO
- 2 LIMES
- 2–3 RIPE SMALL TO MEDIUM AVOCADOS, OR 1–2 LARGE ONES
- ¼– ½ ONION, FINELY CHOPPED
- PINCH OF GROUND CUMIN
- PINCH OF MILD CHILI POWDER
- ½–1 FRESH GREEN CHILE, SUCH AS JALAPEÑO OR SERRANO, SEEDED AND FINELY CHOPPED
- 1 TBSP FINELY CHOPPED FRESH CILANTRO LEAVES, PLUS EXTRA FOR GARNISHING
- SALT (OPTIONAL)
- TORTILLA CHIPS, TO SERVE (OPTIONAL)

1 Place the tomatoes in a heatproof bowl, pour boiling water over to cover, and let them stand for 30 seconds. Drain and plunge into cold water. Peel off the skins. Cut the tomatoes in half, remove the seeds, and chop the flesh.

2 Squeeze the juice from the limes into a small bowl. Cut 1 avocado in half around the pit. Twist the 2 halves apart in opposite directions, then remove the pit with a knife. Carefully peel off the skin, dice the flesh, and toss in the bowl of lime juice to prevent the flesh from discoloring. Repeat with the remaining avocados. Mash the avocado flesh fairly coarsely with a fork.

3 Add the onion, tomato, cumin, chili powder, chopped chile, and fresh cilantro to the avocados. If using as a dip for tortilla chips, do not add salt. If using as a dip for vegetable sticks, add salt to taste.

4 To serve the guacamole, transfer to a serving dish, garnish with finely chopped fresh cilantro, and serve with tortilla chips or vegetable sticks.

CUCUMBER &
TOMATO SOUP

SERVES 6

INGREDIENTS

- 4 TOMATOES, PEELED AND SEEDED
- 3 LB 5 OZ/1.5 KG WATERMELON, SEEDLESS IF AVAILABLE
- 4-INCH/10-CM PIECE CUCUMBER, PEELED AND SEEDED
- 2 SCALLIONS, GREEN PARTS ONLY, CHOPPED
- 1 TBSP CHOPPED FRESH MINT
- SALT AND PEPPER
- FRESH MINT SPRIGS, TO GARNISH

1 Using a sharp knife, cut 1 of the tomatoes into ½-inch/1-cm cubes.

2 Remove the rind from the melon, and remove the seeds if it is not seedless.

3 Put the 3 remaining tomatoes into a blender or food processor and, with the motor running, add the seeded cucumber, chopped scallions, and watermelon. Blend until smooth.

4 If not using a food processor, push the seeded watermelon through a sieve. Stir the diced tomato and mint into the melon mixture. Adjust the seasoning to taste. Chop the cucumber, scallions, and the 3 remaining tomatoes finely and add to the melon.

5 Chill the cucumber and tomato soup overnight in the refrigerator. Check the seasoning and transfer to a serving dish. Garnish with mint sprigs.

TOMATO & ROSEMARY FOCACCIA

MAKES 1 LOAF

INGREDIENTS
- 4¹/₂ CUPS STRONG WHITE BREAD FLOUR, PLUS EXTRA FOR DUSTING
- 1¹/₂ TSP SALT
- 1¹/₂ TSP ACTIVE DRY YEAST
- 2 TBSP CHOPPED FRESH ROSEMARY, PLUS EXTRA SPRIGS TO GARNISH
- 6 TBSP EXTRA VIRGIN OLIVE OIL, PLUS EXTRA FOR BRUSHING
- 1¹/₄ CUPS LUKEWARM WATER
- 6 OVEN-DRIED OR SUN-BLUSH TOMATO HALVES
- 1 TSP COARSE SEA SALT

1 Sift the flour and salt together into a bowl and stir in the yeast and rosemary. Make a well in the center, and pour in 4 tbsp of the olive oil, and mix quickly with a wooden spoon. Gradually stir in the lukewarm water but do not overmix. Turn out onto a lightly floured counter and knead for 2 minutes. The dough will be quite wet; do not add more flour.

2 Brush a bowl with oil. Shape the dough into a ball, put it into the bowl, and put the bowl into a plastic bag or cover with a damp dish towel. Let rise in a warm place for 2 hours, until doubled in volume.

3 Brush a cookie sheet with oil. Turn out the dough onto a lightly floured counter and punch down with your fist, then knead for 1 minute. Put the dough on to the prepared cookie sheet and press out into an even layer. Put the cookie sheet into a plastic bag or cover with a damp dish towel. Let rise in a warm place for 1 hour.

4 Preheat the oven to 475°F/240°C. Cut the tomato halves in half. Whisk the remaining oil with a little water in a bowl. Dip your fingers into the oil mixture and press them into the dough to make dimples all over the loaf. Sprinkle with the sea salt. Press the tomato quarters into some of the dimples, drizzle with the remaining oil mixture, and sprinkle the loaf with the rosemary sprigs.

5 Lower the oven temperature to 425°F/220°C and bake the focaccia for 20 minutes, until golden brown. Transfer to a wire rack to cool slightly, then serve while still warm. Alternatively, let the loaf cool completely and reheat in a low oven before serving.

BELL PEPPERS WITH FETA

MAKES 12

INGREDIENTS
- 4½ OZ/125 G FETA CHEESE (DRAINED WEIGHT)
- 12 LONG, SLENDER RED OR YELLOW BELL PEPPERS OR SHORT, THICK FRESH RED CHILES, RUBBED WITH OLIVE OIL
- EXTRA VIRGIN OLIVE OIL, FOR DRIZZLING
- PEPPER

1 Put the feta cheese in a bowl with warm water to cover. Let the feta soak for 1 hour, changing the water 2–3 times.

2 Meanwhile, preheat the broiler to its highest setting. Put the bell peppers in a broiler pan and cook under the broiler, about 4 inches/10 cm from the heat, for 10 minutes, turning once, until the skins are just charred. Transfer to a bowl, cover with a folded clean dish towel, and cool.

3 When cool enough to handle, peel away the skins, then cut off the tips so that they are about 1½ inches/4 cm long. Use a teaspoon to scrape out the seeds and membranes from the bell pepper tips, being careful not to tear the flesh.

4 Drain the feta cheese well, put in a bowl, and use a fork to mash into a thick paste. Put 1 teaspoon of the cheese in each bell pepper tip and use your fingers to push it into the cavity, handling gently to prevent tearing. Arrange on a serving plate, drizzle with oil, and season to taste with pepper. Cover and chill in the refrigerator until ready to serve.

TOMATO & POTATO TORTILLA

SERVES 6

INGREDIENTS

- 2 LB 4 OZ/1 KG POTATOES, PEELED AND CUT INTO SMALL CUBES
- 2 TBSP OLIVE OIL
- 1 BUNCH OF SCALLIONS, CHOPPED
- 4 OZ/115 G CHERRY TOMATOES, HALVED
- 6 EGGS
- 3 TBSP WATER
- 2 TBSP CHOPPED FRESH PARSLEY
- SALT AND PEPPER

1 Cook the potatoes in a saucepan of lightly salted boiling water for 8–10 minutes, or until tender. Drain and set aside until required.

2 Preheat the broiler to medium. Heat the oil in a large skillet with a heatproof handle. Add the scallions and cook until just softened. Add the potatoes and cook for 3–4 minutes, until coated with oil and hot. Smooth the top and sprinkle the tomatoes throughout.

3 Mix the eggs, water, parsley, and seasoning in a bowl, then pour into the skillet. Cook over very gentle heat for 10–15 minutes, until the tortilla looks fairly set.

4 Place the skillet under the hot broiler and cook until the top is brown and set. Cool for 10–15 minutes before sliding out of the skillet onto a cutting board. Cut into wedges and serve at once.

PASTA SALAD WITH CHARBROILED BELL PEPPERS

SERVES 4

INGREDIENTS
- 1 RED BELL PEPPER
- 1 ORANGE BELL PEPPER
- 10 OZ/280 G DRIED CONCHIGLIE
- 5 TBSP EXTRA VIRGIN OLIVE OIL
- 2 TBSP LEMON JUICE
- 2 TBSP GREEN PESTO
- 1 GARLIC CLOVE, FINELY CHOPPED
- 3 TBSP SHREDDED FRESH BASIL LEAVES
- SALT AND PEPPER

1 Preheat the broiler. Put the whole bell peppers on a baking sheet and place under the hot broiler, turning frequently, for 15 minutes, or until charred all over. Remove with tongs and place in a bowl. Cover with crumpled paper towels and reserve.

2 Meanwhile, bring a large saucepan of lightly salted water to a boil. Add the pasta, return to a boil, and cook for 8–10 minutes, or until tender but still firm to the bite.

3 Combine the olive oil, lemon juice, pesto, and garlic in a bowl, whisking well to mix. Drain the pasta, add it to the pesto mixture while still hot, and toss well. Reserve until required.

4 When the bell peppers are cool enough to handle, peel off the skins, then cut open and remove the seeds. Chop the flesh coarsely and add to the pasta with the basil. Season to taste with salt and pepper and toss well. Serve.

ZUCCHINI & BASIL RISOTTO

SERVES 4

INGREDIENTS

- 4 TBSP BASIL-FLAVORED EXTRA VIRGIN OLIVE OIL, PLUS EXTRA FOR DRIZZLING
- 4 ZUCCHINI, DICED
- 1 YELLOW BELL PEPPER, SEEDED AND DICED
- 2 GARLIC CLOVES, FINELY CHOPPED
- 1 LARGE ONION, FINELY CHOPPED
- 3½ CUPS RISOTTO RICE
- 4 TBSP DRY WHITE VERMOUTH
- SCANT 7 CUPS VEGETABLE STOCK, SIMMERING
- 2 TBSP UNSALTED BUTTER, AT ROOM TEMPERATURE
- LARGE HANDFUL OF FRESH BASIL LEAVES, TORN, PLUS A FEW LEAVES TO GARNISH
- 1 CUP FRESHLY GRATED PARMESAN CHEESE

1 Heat half the oil in a large skillet over high heat. When very hot, but not smoking, add the zucchini and yellow bell pepper and stir-fry for 3 minutes, until lightly golden. Stir in the garlic and cook for about 30 seconds longer. Transfer to a plate and set aside.

2 Heat the remaining oil in a large heavy pan over medium heat. Add the onion and cook, stirring occasionally, for about 2 minutes, until soft. Add the rice and cook, stirring frequently, for about 2 minutes, until the rice is translucent and well coated with the olive oil.

3 Pour in the vermouth; it will bubble and steam rapidly and evaporate almost immediately. Add a ladleful (about ½ cup) of the simmering stock and cook, stirring constantly, until the stock is completely absorbed.

4 Continue adding the stock, about half a ladleful at a time, letting each addition be absorbed before adding the next. This should take 20–25 minutes. The risotto should have a creamy consistency and the rice should be tender, but still firm to the bite.

5 Stir in the zucchini mixture with any juices, and the butter, basil, and grated Parmesan. Drizzle with a little oil and garnish with basil. Serve hot.

PASTA ALL'ARRABBIATA

SERVES 4

INGREDIENTS
- ⅔ CUP DRY WHITE WINE
- 1 TBSP SUN-DRIED TOMATO PASTE
- 2 FRESH RED CHILES
- 2 GARLIC CLOVES, FINELY CHOPPED
- 12 OZ/350 G DRIED TORTIGLIONI
- 4 TBSP CHOPPED FRESH FLAT-LEAF PARSLEY
- SALT AND PEPPER
- FRESH ROMANO CHEESE SHAVINGS, TO GARNISH

SUGOCASA
- 5 TBSP EXTRA VIRGIN OLIVE OIL
- 1 LB/450 G PLUM TOMATOES, CHOPPED
- SALT AND PEPPER

1 To make the sugocasa, heat the oil in a skillet over high heat until almost smoking. Add the tomatoes and cook, stirring frequently, for 2–3 minutes. Reduce the heat to low and cook gently for 20 minutes, or until very soft. Season to taste with salt and pepper. Press through a nonmetallic sieve with a wooden spoon into a saucepan.

2 Add the wine, tomato paste, whole chiles, and garlic to the sugocasa, and bring to a boil. Reduce the heat and simmer gently.

3 Meanwhile, bring a large saucepan of lightly salted water to a boil. Add the pasta, return to a boil, and cook for 8–10 minutes, until tender but still firm to the bite.

4 Remove the chiles and taste the sauce. If you prefer a hotter flavor, chop some or all of the chiles and return to the pan. Check and adjust the seasoning, if necessary, then stir in half the parsley.

5 Drain the pasta and transfer to a warmed serving bowl. Add the sauce and toss to coat. Sprinkle with the remaining parsley, garnish with the Romano cheese shavings, and serve immediately.

CHILI TOFU TORTILLAS

MAKES 8

INGREDIENTS

- ½ TSP CHILI POWDER
- 1 TSP PAPRIKA
- 2 TBSP ALL-PURPOSE FLOUR
- 8 OZ/225 G TOFU, CUT INTO ½ INCH/1 CM PIECES
- 2 TBSP VEGETABLE OIL
- 1 ONION, FINELY CHOPPED
- 1 GARLIC CLOVE, CRUSHED
- 1 LARGE RED BELL PEPPER, SEEDED AND FINELY CHOPPED
- 1 LARGE RIPE AVOCADO
- 1 TBSP LIME JUICE
- 4 TOMATOES, PEELED, SEEDED, AND CHOPPED
- 1 CUP GRATED CHEDDAR CHEESE
- 8 SOFT FLOUR TORTILLAS
- ⅔ CUP SOUR CREAM
- SALT AND PEPPER
- CILANTRO SPRIGS, TO GARNISH
- PICKLED GREEN JALAPEÑO CHILES, TO SERVE

SAUCE

- 3½ CUPS SUGOCASA
- 3 TBSP CHOPPED FRESH PARSLEY
- 3 TBSP CHOPPED FRESH CILANTRO

1 Preheat the oven to 375°F/190°C. Mix the chili powder, paprika, flour, and seasoning on a plate and use to coat the tofu pieces.

2 Heat the oil in a skillet and gently cook the tofu for 3–4 minutes, until golden. Remove with a slotted spoon, drain on paper towels, and set aside.

3 Add the onion, garlic, and bell pepper to the oil and cook for 2–3 minutes, until just soft. Drain and set aside.

4 Halve the avocado, peel, and remove the pit. Slice lengthwise, put in a bowl with the lime juice, and toss to coat.

5 Add the tofu and onion mixture and gently stir in the chopped tomatoes and half the grated Cheddar cheese. Spoon one-eighth of the filling down the center of each tortilla, top with sour cream, and roll up.

6 Arrange the tortillas, seam-sides down, in a shallow ovenproof dish in a single layer.

7 To make the sauce, mix together all the ingredients. Spoon the sauce over the tortillas, sprinkle with the remaining grated cheese, and bake in the preheated oven for 25 minutes, until the cheese is golden brown and bubbling.

8 Garnish the chili tofu with cilantro sprigs and serve immediately with pickled jalapeño chiles.

PASTA SHAPES WITH PUMPKIN SAUCE

SERVES 4

INGREDIENTS

- 4 TBSP UNSALTED BUTTER
- 4 OZ/115 G WHITE ONIONS OR SHALLOTS, VERY FINELY CHOPPED
- 1 LB 12 OZ/800 G PUMPKIN, UNPREPARED WEIGHT
- PINCH OF FRESHLY GRATED NUTMEG
- 12 OZ/350 G DRIED PENNE OR RADIATORE
- GENEROUS ¾ CUP LIGHT CREAM
- 4 TBSP FRESHLY GRATED PARMESAN CHEESE, PLUS EXTRA TO SERVE
- 2 TBSP CHOPPED FRESH FLAT-LEAF PARSLEY
- SALT AND PEPPER

1 Melt the butter in a heavy-bottom saucepan over low heat. Add the onions, sprinkle with a little salt, cover, and cook, stirring frequently, for 25–30 minutes.

2 Scoop out and discard the seeds from the pumpkin. Peel and finely chop the flesh. Tip the pumpkin into the saucepan and season to taste with nutmeg. Cover and cook over low heat, stirring occasionally, for 45 minutes.

3 Meanwhile, bring a large saucepan of lightly salted water to a boil. Add the pasta, return to a boil, and cook for 8–10 minutes, or until tender but still firm to the bite. Drain thoroughly, reserving about $^2/_3$ cup of the cooking liquid.

4 Stir the cream, grated Parmesan cheese, and parsley into the pumpkin sauce and season to taste with salt and pepper. If the mixture seems a little too thick, add some or all of the reserved cooking liquid and stir. Tip in the pasta and toss for 1 minute. Serve immediately, with extra Parmesan cheese for sprinkling.

PUMPKIN CHESTNUT RISOTTO

SERVES 4

INGREDIENTS

- 4 CUPS VEGETABLE STOCK OR CHICKEN STOCK
- 1 TBSP OLIVE OIL
- 3 TBSP BUTTER
- 1 SMALL ONION, FINELY CHOPPED
- SCANT 1½ CUPS PUMPKIN, DICED
- 8 OZ/225 G CHESTNUTS, COOKED AND SHELLED
- GENEROUS 1⅜ CUPS RISOTTO RICE
- ⅔ CUP DRY WHITE WINE
- 1 TSP CRUMBLED SAFFRON THREADS (OPTIONAL)
- ¾ CUP FRESHLY GRATED PARMESAN OR GRANA PADANO CHEESE
- SALT AND PEPPER

1 Bring the stock to a boil, then reduce the heat and keep simmering gently over low heat while you are cooking the risotto.

2 Heat the oil with 2 tablespoons of the butter in a deep pan over medium heat until the butter has melted. Stir in the onion and pumpkin and cook, stirring occasionally, for 5 minutes, or until the onion is soft and starting to turn golden and the pumpkin begins to color. Coarsely chop the chestnuts and add to the mixture. Stir thoroughly to coat.

3 Reduce the heat, add the rice, and mix to coat in oil and butter. Cook, stirring constantly, for 2–3 minutes, or until the grains are translucent. Add the wine and cook, stirring constantly, for 1 minute, until it has reduced. If using the saffron threads, dissolve them in 4 tablespoons of the hot stock and add the liquid to the rice after the wine has been absorbed. Cook, stirring constantly, until the liquid has been absorbed.

4 Gradually add the hot stock, a ladleful at a time. Stir constantly and add more liquid as the rice absorbs each addition. Increase the heat to medium so that the liquid bubbles. Cook for 20 minutes, or until all the liquid is absorbed and the rice is creamy. Season to taste.

5 Remove the risotto from the heat and add the remaining butter. Mix well, then stir in the Parmesan until it melts. Adjust the seasoning if necessary, spoon the risotto onto 4 warmed plates, and serve at once.

BUTTERNUT SQUASH
STIR-FRY

SERVES 4

INGREDIENTS

- 2 LB/900 G BUTTERNUT SQUASH, PEELED
- 3 TBSP PEANUT OIL
- 1 ONION, SLICED
- 2 GARLIC CLOVES, CRUSHED
- 1 TSP CORIANDER SEEDS
- 1 TSP CUMIN SEEDS
- 2 TBSP CHOPPED FRESH CILANTRO
- GENEROUS ⅓ CUP COCONUT MILK
- ½ CUP WATER
- ⅔ CUP SALTED CASHEWS

TO GARNISH

- FRESHLY GRATED LIME ZEST
- FRESH CILANTRO
- LIME HALVES

1 Slice the butternut squash into small, bite-size cubes, using a sharp knife.

2 Heat the peanut oil in a large preheated wok.

3 Add the butternut squash, onion, and garlic and cook for 5 minutes.

4 Stir in the coriander seeds, cumin seeds, and fresh cilantro and cook for 1 minute.

5 Add the coconut milk and water to the wok and bring to a boil. Cover the wok and simmer for 10–15 minutes, or until the squash is tender.

6 Add the cashews and stir to combine. Transfer the stir-fry to warm serving dishes and garnish with freshly grated lime zest, fresh cilantro, and lime halves. Serve hot.

STUFFED EGGPLANTS

SERVES 4

INGREDIENTS

- 2 CUPS DRIED PENNE OR OTHER SHORT PASTA SHAPES
- 4 TBSP OLIVE OIL, PLUS EXTRA FOR BRUSHING
- 2 EGGPLANTS
- 1 LARGE ONION, CHOPPED
- 2 GARLIC CLOVES, CRUSHED
- 14 OZ/400 G CANNED CHOPPED TOMATOES
- 2 TSP DRIED OREGANO
- 2 OZ/55 G MOZZARELLA CHEESE, THINLY SLICED
- ⅓ CUP FRESHLY GRATED PARMESAN CHEESE
- 5 TBSP DRY BREADCRUMBS
- SALT AND PEPPER

1 Preheat the oven to 400°F/200°C. Bring a large saucepan of lightly salted water to a boil. Add the pasta and 1 tablespoon of the olive oil, bring back to a boil, and cook for 8–10 minutes, or until the pasta is just tender but still firm to the bite. Drain, return to the saucepan, cover, and keep warm.

2 Cut the eggplants in half lengthwise and score around the insides with a sharp knife, being careful not to pierce the shells. Scoop out the flesh with a spoon. Brush the insides of the shells with olive oil. Chop the flesh and set aside.

3 Heat the remaining oil in a skillet. Cook the onion over low heat for 5 minutes, until softened. Add the garlic and cook for 1 minute. Add the chopped eggplant and cook, stirring frequently, for 5 minutes. Add the tomatoes and oregano and season to taste with salt and pepper. Bring to a boil and simmer for 10 minutes, until thickened. Remove the skillet from the heat and stir in the pasta.

4 Brush a baking sheet with oil and arrange the eggplant shells in a single layer. Divide half of the tomato and pasta mixture among them. Sprinkle over the slices of mozzarella, then pile the remaining tomato and pasta mixture on top. Mix the Parmesan cheese and breadcrumbs and sprinkle over the top, patting lightly into the mixture.

5 Bake in the preheated oven for approximately 25 minutes or until the topping is golden brown.

EGGPLANT CURRY

SERVES 2

INGREDIENTS

- 2 TBSP PEANUT OIL OR VEGETABLE OIL, PLUS EXTRA FOR DEEP-FRYING
- 2 EGGPLANTS, CUT INTO ¾-INCH/2-CM CUBES
- 1 BUNCH OF SCALLIONS, COARSELY CHOPPED
- 2 GARLIC CLOVES, CHOPPED
- 2 RED BELL PEPPERS, SEEDED AND CUT INTO ¾-INCH/2-CM SQUARES
- 3 ZUCCHINI, THICKLY SLICED
- 1¾ CUPS CANNED COCONUT MILK
- 2 TBSP RED CURRY PASTE
- LARGE HANDFUL OF FRESH CILANTRO, CHOPPED, PLUS EXTRA SPRIGS, TO GARNISH
- COOKED RICE OR NOODLES, TO SERVE

1 Heat the oil for deep-frying in a preheated wok or a deep pan or deep-fat fryer to 350–375°F/180–190°C, or until a cube of bread browns in 30 seconds. Add the eggplant cubes, in batches, and cook for 45 seconds to 1 minute, or until crisp and brown all over. Remove with a slotted spoon and drain on paper towels.

2 Heat the remaining 2 tablespoons of oil in a separate preheated wok or large skillet. Add the scallions and garlic and stir-fry over medium–high heat for 1 minute. Add the red bell peppers and zucchini and stir-fry for 2–3 minutes. Add the coconut milk and curry paste and bring gently to a boil, stirring occasionally. Add the eggplants and cilantro, then reduce the heat and simmer for 2–3 minutes.

3 Serve immediately with rice or noodles, garnished with cilantro sprigs.

CORNMEAL WITH TOMATOES & GARLIC SAUCE

SERVES 4

INGREDIENTS
- 3 CUPS VEGETABLE STOCK OR WATER
- 1½ CUPS QUICK-COOK CORNMEAL
- 2 TBSP BUTTER
- 3 TBSP SNIPPED FRESH CHIVES
- 2 TBSP CHOPPED FRESH FLAT-LEAF PARSLEY
- OLIVE OIL, FOR BRUSHING
- 4 PLUM TOMATOES, SLICED
- SALT AND PEPPER

GARLIC SAUCE
- 2 THICK SLICES OF FRENCH BREAD, CRUSTS REMOVED
- 3 GARLIC CLOVES, CHOPPED
- 1 CUP WALNUT PIECES
- 3 TBSP LEMON JUICE
- SCANT ½ CUP OLIVE OIL

1 Bring the stock to a boil in a large saucepan and add 1 teaspoon salt. Add the cornmeal and cook over medium heat, stirring constantly, for 5 minutes, until it starts to come away from the side of the saucepan.

2 Remove the saucepan from the heat and beat in the butter, chives, and parsley, and season with pepper. Pour the cornmeal into a greased dish and spread out evenly. Let the cornmeal cool and set.

3 To make the sauce, tear the bread into pieces and place in a bowl. Cover with cold water and soak for 10 minutes. Pound the garlic cloves with ½ teaspoon salt to make a paste. Work in the walnuts. Squeeze out the bread, work it into the paste, then work in the lemon juice. Stir in the olive oil until the sauce is thick and creamy, then transfer to a bowl, cover with plastic wrap, and set aside.

4 Brush a grill pan with oil and preheat. Cut the set cornmeal into wedges or rounds. Season the tomatoes with salt and pepper. When the grill pan is hot, add the cornmeal and tomatoes and cook for 4–5 minutes.

5 Divide the cornmeal and tomatoes among warm plates and spoon over the sauce. Serve immediately.

3

MUSHROOMS & THE ONION FAMILY

If you've fallen into the habit of simply sautéeing chopped onion to flavor other ingredients, the recipes in this chapter should make you reconsider your attitude. Like other roots, members of the onion family respond to many culinary treatments and make excellent soups, pasta sauces, and Indian-style dishes. Once rare, wild mushrooms are now readily available so use the recipes in this chapter to try a new variety—most are interchangeable so you can always try an alternative type.

DIRECTORY OF MUSHROOMS & ONIONS

The onion has traditionally been used to provide a basis for many recipes, although, as this chapter shows, it really comes into its own when served as a vegetable in its own right. The extremely versatile mushroom can be eaten raw in salads, cooked as a vegetable accompaniment, or used to flavor a variety of dishes ranging from soups to risottos.

Mushrooms

There is a wide range of mushrooms from which to choose, both fresh and dried, and many types of wild mushroom are now cultivated. The most popular are the mild-flavored button mushroom and the portobello mushroom, which has a more earthy, intense flavor. Buy mushrooms that are firm and smell fresh; avoid ones that have slimy, damp patches. Dried mushrooms keep well: to reconstitute them, soak in boiling water for 20–30 minutes. Drain and rinse well to remove any dirt and grit. Use the soaking water in stocks and sauces, but strain first.

Porcini

Porcini mushrooms have a meaty texture and woody flavor. Dried porcini lend a rich flavor to soups, stocks, and sauces.

Chanterelle

Golden-colored chanterelle (or girolle) mushrooms have a delicate flavor. They should be wiped instead of washed because they are very porous. Most types of mushroom should be prepared in this way, apart from the honeycomb-capped morel.

Shiitake and oyster

Both shiitake and oyster mushrooms are now widely cultivated. Oyster are fluted in shape, and while they are usually grayish brown in color, they also come in pale yellow and pink. Shiitake have a chewy texture and robust flavor, and are most commonly used in Asian dishes.

Onion family

Onions, garlic, leeks, shallots, and scallions add plenty of flavor to all manner of savory vegetarian dishes and can also be cooked on their own. Onions and garlic should be stored in a cool, dry, airy place away from direct sunlight.

Onions

These provide potent antioxidants and are said to reduce health-threatening cholesterol levels in the body. Cooking tempers the pungency of the onion family, while roasting brings out their delicious sweetness. Onions offer a range of taste sensations, from the sweet and mild Spanish white onion and the light and fresh scallion, to the versatile and pungent yellow onion. Pearl onions and shallots are the smallest.

WILD MUSHROOM BRUSCHETTA

SERVES 4

INGREDIENTS

- 4 SLICES SOURDOUGH BREAD, SUCH AS PUGLIESE
- 3 GARLIC CLOVES, 1 HALVED AND 2 CRUSHED
- 2 TBSP EXTRA VIRGIN OLIVE OIL
- 8 OZ/225 G MIXED WILD MUSHROOMS, SUCH AS PORCINI, CHANTERELLES, AND PORTOBELLO MUSHROOMS
- 1 TBSP OLIVE OIL
- 2 TBSP BUTTER
- 1 SMALL ONION OR 2 SHALLOTS, FINELY CHOPPED
- ¼ CUP DRY WHITE WINE OR MARSALA
- SALT AND PEPPER
- 2 TBSP COARSELY CHOPPED FRESH FLAT-LEAF PARSLEY, TO GARNISH

1 Toast the bread slices under a preheated broiler or in a preheated ridged grill pan on both sides, then rub with the garlic halves and drizzle with the extra virgin olive oil. Transfer to a baking sheet and keep warm in a warm oven.

2 Wipe the mushrooms thoroughly to remove any trace of soil, and slice any large ones. Heat the olive oil with half the butter in a skillet, then add the mushrooms and cook over medium heat, stirring frequently, for 3–4 minutes, or until soft. Remove with a slotted spoon and keep warm in the oven.

3 Heat the remaining butter in the skillet and add the onion and crushed garlic, then cook over medium heat, stirring frequently, for 3–4 minutes, or until soft. Add the wine and stir well, then let the mixture bubble for 2–3 minutes, or until reduced and thickened. Return the mushrooms to the skillet and heat through. The sauce should be thick enough to glaze the mushrooms. Season to taste with salt and pepper.

4 Pile the mushrooms on top of the warm bruschetta, then sprinkle with the parsley and serve immediately.

MUSHROOM PASTA WITH PORT

SERVES 4

INGREDIENTS
- 4 TBSP BUTTER
- 2 TBSP OLIVE OIL
- 6 SHALLOTS, SLICED
- 6 CUPS SLICED WHITE MUSHROOMS
- 1 TSP ALL-PURPOSE FLOUR
- SCANT ¾ CUP HEAVY CREAM
- 2 TBSP PORT
- 4 OZ/115 G SUN-DRIED TOMATOES, CHOPPED
- FRESHLY GRATED NUTMEG
- 1 LB/450 G DRIED SPAGHETTI
- 1 TBSP CHOPPED FRESH PARSLEY
- SALT AND PEPPER
- 6 TRIANGLES OF FRIED WHITE BREAD, TO SERVE

1 Heat the butter and half of the olive oil in a large saucepan. Add the shallots and cook over medium heat for 3 minutes. Add the mushrooms and cook over low heat for 2 minutes. Season to taste with salt and black pepper, then sprinkle over the flour and cook, stirring constantly, for 1 minute.

2 Gradually stir in the cream and port, then add the sun-dried tomatoes and a pinch of grated nutmeg, and cook over low heat for 8 minutes.

3 Meanwhile, bring a large saucepan of lightly salted water to a boil. Add the spaghetti and remaining olive oil and cook for 12–14 minutes, or until tender but still firm to the bite.

4 Drain the spaghetti and return to the pan. Pour over the mushroom sauce and cook for 3 minutes. Transfer the spaghetti and mushroom sauce to a large serving plate and sprinkle over the chopped parsley. Serve with triangles of crispy fried bread.

PARMESAN CHEESE RISOTTO WITH MUSHROOMS

SERVES 4

INGREDIENTS

- 4 CUPS VEGETABLE STOCK OR CHICKEN STOCK
- 2 TBSP OLIVE OIL OR VEGETABLE OIL
- GENEROUS 1 CUP RISOTTO RICE
- 2 GARLIC CLOVES, CRUSHED
- 1 ONION, CHOPPED
- 2 CELERY STALKS, CHOPPED
- 1 RED OR GREEN BELL PEPPER, SEEDED AND CHOPPED
- 8 OZ/225 G MUSHROOMS, THINLY SLICED
- 1 TBSP CHOPPED FRESH OREGANO OR 1 TSP DRIED OREGANO
- ¼ CUP SUN-DRIED TOMATOES IN OLIVE OIL, DRAINED AND CHOPPED (OPTIONAL)
- ½ CUP FINELY GRATED PARMESAN CHEESE
- SALT AND PEPPER
- FRESH FLAT-LEAF PARSLEY SPRIGS OR FRESH BAY LEAVES, TO GARNISH

1 Bring the stock to a boil in a saucepan, then reduce the heat and keep simmering gently over low heat while you are cooking the risotto.

2 Heat the oil in a deep skillet or saucepan. Add the rice and cook over low heat, stirring constantly, for 2–3 minutes, until the grains are thoroughly coated in oil and translucent.

3 Add the garlic, onion, celery, and bell pepper and cook, stirring frequently, for 5 minutes. Add the mushrooms and cook for 3–4 minutes. Stir in the oregano.

4 Gradually add the hot stock, a ladleful at a time. Stir constantly and add more liquid as the rice absorbs each addition. Increase the heat to medium so that the liquid bubbles. Cook for 20 minutes, or until all the liquid is absorbed and the rice is creamy. Add the sun-dried tomatoes, if using, 5 minutes before the end of the cooking time and season to taste with salt and pepper.

5 Remove the risotto from the heat and stir in half the Parmesan cheese until it melts. Transfer the risotto to warmed plates. Top with the remaining cheese, garnish with flat-leaf parsley or bay leaves, and serve at once.

MIXED MUSHROOM PIZZA

**MAKES TWO 9-INCH/
23-CM PIZZAS**

INGREDIENTS

- 3 TBSP OIL
- 2 GARLIC CLOVES, CRUSHED
- 2 TBSP CHOPPED FRESH OREGANO
- TWO 9-INCH/23-CM PREPARED THIN AND CRISPY PIZZA BASES
- ¾ CUP CURD CHEESE
- 1 TBSP MILK
- 3 TBSP BUTTER
- 12 OZ/350 G MIXED MUSHROOMS, SLICED
- 2 TSP LEMON JUICE
- 1 TBSP CHOPPED FRESH MARJORAM
- 4 TBSP FRESHLY GRATED PARMESAN CHEESE
- SALT AND PEPPER

1 Preheat the oven to 475°F/240°C. Mix 2 tablespoons of the oil, and the garlic and oregano, and brush over the pizza bases.

2 Mix the curd cheese and milk together in a bowl. Season to taste with salt and pepper and spread the mixture over the pizza bases, leaving a 1¹/₂-inch/4-cm border.

3 Heat the butter and remaining oil together in a large skillet. Add the mushrooms and cook over high heat for 2 minutes. Remove the skillet from the heat, season to taste with salt and pepper, and stir in the lemon juice and marjoram.

4 Spoon the mushroom mixture over the pizza bases, leaving a ½-inch/ 1-cm border. Sprinkle with the grated Parmesan cheese, then bake in the oven for 12–15 minutes, until the crusts are crisp and the mushrooms are cooked. Serve at once.

RED ONION, TOMATO & HERB SALAD

SERVES 4

INGREDIENTS

- 2 LB/900 G TOMATOES, THINLY SLICED
- 1 TBSP SUGAR (OPTIONAL)
- 1 RED ONION, THINLY SLICED
- LARGE HANDFUL OF COARSELY CHOPPED FRESH HERBS, USING ANY IN SEASON, SUCH AS TARRAGON, SORREL, CILANTRO, OR BASIL
- SALT AND PEPPER

DRESSING

- 2–4 TBSP VEGETABLE OIL
- 2 TBSP RED WINE VINEGAR OR FRUIT VINEGAR

1 Arrange the tomato slices in a shallow bowl. Sprinkle with sugar (if using), and salt and pepper.

2 Separate the onion slices into rings and sprinkle them over the tomatoes. Sprinkle the chopped fresh herbs over the top.

3 Place the dressing ingredients in a jar with a screw-top lid. Shake well. Pour the dressing over the salad and mix gently.

4 Cover with plastic wrap and chill for 20 minutes. Remove the salad from the refrigerator 5 minutes before serving, unwrap the dish, and stir gently before setting out on the table.

FLATBREAD WITH ONION & ROSEMARY

MAKES 1 LOAF

INGREDIENTS

- 1 LB/450 G WHITE BREAD FLOUR, PLUS EXTRA FOR DUSTING
- 1½ TSP ACTIVE DRY YEAST
- ½ TSP SALT
- 2 TBSP CHOPPED FRESH ROSEMARY, PLUS EXTRA SMALL SPRIGS TO GARNISH
- 5 TBSP EXTRA VIRGIN OLIVE OIL, PLUS EXTRA FOR OILING
- 1¼ CUPS WARM WATER
- 1 RED ONION, FINELY SLICED AND SEPARATED INTO RINGS
- 1 TBSP COARSE SEA SALT

1 Mix the flour, yeast, and salt together in a mixing bowl, then stir in the chopped rosemary. Make a well in the center. Mix 3 tablespoons of the oil and all the water in a pitcher and pour into the well. Gradually mix the liquid into the flour mixture with a round-bladed knife. Gather the mixture together with your hands to form a soft dough.

2 Turn the dough out onto a lightly floured counter and then knead for 8–10 minutes, or until very smooth and elastic. Return the dough to the bowl and cover with a clean dish towel or oiled plastic wrap, then let the dough rise in a warm place for ¾ –1 hour, or until doubled in size. Turn out and gently knead again for 1 minute, or until smooth.

3 Preheat the oven to 400°F/200°C. Oil a cookie sheet. Gently roll the dough out to a circle about 12 inches/30 cm in diameter—it doesn't have to be a perfect circle; a slightly oval shape is traditional. Transfer to the prepared cookie sheet and cover with a clean dish towel or oiled plastic wrap, then let the dough rise in a warm place for 20–30 minutes.

4 Make holes about 2 inches/5 cm apart all over the surface of the dough with the handle of a wooden spoon. Spread the onion rings over the dough, then drizzle with the remaining oil and sprinkle over the salt. Bake the dough in the preheated oven for 20–25 minutes, or until well risen and golden brown. Five minutes before the end of the cooking time, garnish with the rosemary sprigs. Transfer to a cooling rack to cool for a few minutes, then serve the bread warm.

CARAMELIZED ONION TART

SERVES 4–6

INGREDIENTS

- SCANT ½ CUP UNSALTED BUTTER
- 1 LB 5 OZ/600 G ONIONS, THINLY SLICED
- 2 EGGS
- GENEROUS ⅓ CUP HEAVY CREAM
- ⅞ CUP GRATED GRUYÈRE CHEESE
- 8-INCH/20-CM PREBAKED PASTRY SHELL
- ⅞ CUP COARSELY GRATED PARMESAN CHEESE
- SALT AND PEPPER

1 Melt the butter in a heavy-bottom skillet over medium heat. Add the onions and cook, stirring frequently to avoid burning, for 30 minutes, or until well-browned and caramelized. Remove the onions from the skillet and set aside.

2 Preheat the oven to 375°F/190°C. Beat the eggs in a large bowl, stir in the cream, and season to taste with salt and pepper. Add the Gruyère and mix well. Stir in the cooked onions.

3 Pour the egg and onion mixture into the baked pastry shell and sprinkle with the Parmesan cheese. Put on a baking sheet. Bake in the preheated oven for 15–20 minutes, until the filling has set and begun to brown.

4 Remove from the oven and let the tart rest for at least 10 minutes. The tart can be served hot or left to cool to room temperature.

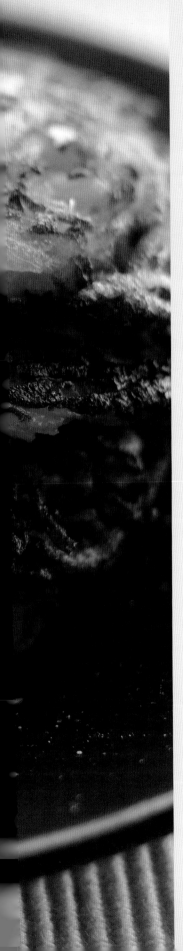

VEGETABLE CAKES

SERVES 4

INGREDIENTS
- 1 LB/450 G STARCHY POTATOES
- 1 MEDIUM ONION, GRATED
- SALT AND PEPPER
- OIL FOR SHALLOW FRYING

1 Wash the potatoes, but do not peel them. Place them in a large saucepan, cover with water, and bring to a boil, covered, over high heat. Reduce the heat and simmer for about 10 minutes, until the potatoes are just beginning to soften. Be careful not to overcook.

2 Drain the potatoes. Cool, then peel, and grate coarsely. Mix the grated onion with the potatoes. Season the mixture with salt and pepper.

3 Heat the oil in a heavy skillet and spoon in the potato mixture. The vegetable cakes can be as thick or as thin as you like, and can be made into 1 large cake or several individual ones.

4 Cook over high heat for about 5 minutes, until the bottom is golden, then turn, and cook until the second side is brown and crispy. Remove from the heat, drain, and then serve.

ONION DAL

SERVES 4

INGREDIENTS

- ½ CUP MASOOR DAL
- 6 TBSP VEGETABLE OIL
- 1 SMALL BUNCH SCALLIONS, CHOPPED
- 1 TSP FINELY CHOPPED FRESH GINGER
- 1 TSP CRUSHED GARLIC
- ½ TSP CHILI POWDER
- ½ TSP TURMERIC
- 1¼ CUPS WATER
- 1 TSP SALT
- 1 FRESH GREEN CHILE, FINELY CHOPPED, AND FRESH CILANTRO LEAVES, TO GARNISH

1 Rinse the lentils thoroughly and set aside until required.

2 Heat the oil in a heavy pan. Add the scallions to the pan and cook over medium heat, stirring frequently, until lightly browned.

3 Reduce the heat and add the ginger, garlic, chili powder, and turmeric. Briefly stir-fry the scallions with the spices. Add the lentils and stir to blend.

4 Add the water to the lentil mixture, reduce the heat to low, and cook for 20–25 minutes.

5 When the lentils are thoroughly cooked and tender, add the salt and stir gently to mix well.

6 Transfer the onion dal to a serving dish. Garnish with the chopped green chile and fresh cilantro leaves and serve immediately.

LEEK & GOAT CHEESE CRÊPES

MAKES 8

INGREDIENTS

- 2 TBSP UNSALTED BUTTER
- ½ TBSP SUNFLOWER OIL
- 7 OZ/200 G LEEKS, HALVED, RINSED, AND FINELY SHREDDED
- FRESHLY GRATED NUTMEG, TO TASTE
- 1 TBSP FINELY SNIPPED FRESH CHIVES
- 8 SAVORY CRÊPES
- 3 OZ/85 G SOFT GOAT CHEESE, RIND REMOVED IF NECESSARY, CHOPPED
- SALT AND PEPPER

1 Preheat the oven to 400°F/200°C. Melt the butter with the oil in a heavy-bottom saucepan with a lid over medium-high heat. Add the leeks and stir around so that they are well coated. Stir in salt and pepper to taste, but remember the cheese might be salty. Add a few gratings of nutmeg, then cover the leeks with a sheet of wet wax paper and put the lid on the saucepan. Reduce the heat to very low and let the leeks sweat for 5–7 minutes, until very tender but not brown. Stir in the chives, then taste and adjust the seasoning if necessary.

2 Put 1 crêpe on the counter and put one-eighth of the leeks on the crêpe. Top with one-eighth of the cheese, then fold the crêpe into a square pocket or simply roll it around the filling. Place the stuffed crêpe on a baking sheet, then continue to fill and fold, or roll, the remaining crêpes.

3 Put the baking sheet in the oven and bake for 5 minutes, or until the crêpes are hot and the cheese starts to melt. Serve hot.

LEEK & HERB
SOUFFLÉS

MAKES 4

INGREDIENTS
- 12 OZ/350 G BABY LEEKS
- 1 TBSP OLIVE OIL, PLUS EXTRA
  FOR GREASING
- ½ CUP VEGETABLE STOCK
- ½ CUP WALNUTS
- 2 EGGS, SEPARATED
- 2 TBSP CHOPPED MIXED HERBS
- 2 TBSP PLAIN YOGURT
- SALT AND PEPPER

1 Using a sharp knife, chop the leeks finely. Heat the oil in a skillet. Add the leeks and sauté over medium heat, stirring occasionally, for 2–3 minutes.

2 Add the vegetable stock to the skillet, lower the heat, and simmer gently for an additional 5 minutes.

3 Place the walnuts in a food processor and process until finely chopped. Add the leek mixture to the nuts and process briefly to form a puree. Transfer to a mixing bowl.

4 Mix together the egg yolks, the herbs, and the yogurt until thoroughly combined. Pour the egg mixture into the leek puree. Season with salt and pepper to taste and mix well.

5 In a separate, grease-free mixing bowl, whisk the egg whites until firm peaks form.

6 Fold the egg whites into the leek mixture. Spoon the mixture into a lightly greased 1-quart/1-liter soufflé dish or 4 individual soufflé dishes and place on a warmed baking sheet. Cook in a preheated oven, 350°F/180°C, for 35–40 minutes, or until well risen, set, and golden brown on top. Serve immediately.

LEEKS WITH YELLOW BEAN SAUCE

SERVES 4

INGREDIENTS
- 1 LB/450 G LEEKS
- 15 BABY CORN EARS
- 6 SCALLIONS
- 3 TBSP PEANUT OIL
- 8 OZ/225 G CHINESE CABBAGE, SHREDDED
- 4 TBSP YELLOW BEAN SAUCE

1 Using a sharp knife, slice the leeks, halve the baby corn ears, and thinly slice the scallions.

2 Heat the oil in a large preheated wok or skillet until smoking.

3 Add the leeks, shredded Chinese cabbage, and baby corn ears to the pan.

4 Cook the vegetables over high heat for about 5 minutes, or until the edges of the vegetables are slightly brown.

5 Add the sliced scallions to the pan, stirring to combine.

6 Add the yellow bean sauce to the pan and cook the mixture over low heat, stirring occasionally, for an additional 2 minutes, or until the vegetables are heated through and thoroughly coated in the sauce.

7 Transfer the vegetables and sauce to warm serving dishes and serve immediately.

CHILLED GARLIC SOUP

SERVES 4–6

INGREDIENTS

- 1 LB 2 OZ/500 G DAY-OLD COUNTRY-STYLE WHITE BREAD, CRUSTS REMOVED, THEN TORN
- 5 LARGE GARLIC CLOVES, HALVED
- ½ CUP EXTRA VIRGIN OLIVE OIL, PLUS A LITTLE EXTRA, TO GARNISH
- 4–5 TBSP SHERRY VINEGAR, TO TASTE
- 3⅛ CUP GROUND ALMONDS
- 5 CUPS WATER, CHILLED
- SALT AND WHITE PEPPER
- SEEDLESS WHITE GRAPES, TO GARNISH

1 Put the bread in a bowl with just enough cold water to cover and soak for 15 minutes. Squeeze the bread dry and transfer it to a food processor.

2 Add the garlic, oil, 4 tablespoons of sherry vinegar, and the ground almonds to the food processor with 1 cup of the water and process until blended.

3 With the motor running, slowly pour in the remaining water until a smooth soup forms. Taste and add extra sherry vinegar if necessary. Cover with plastic wrap and chill for at least 4 hours.

4 To serve, stir well and adjust the seasoning if necessary. Ladle into bowls and float grapes on top with a drizzle of olive oil.

ROAST GARLIC WITH GOAT CHEESE

SERVES 4

INGREDIENTS

- 2 GARLIC BULBS, OUTER PAPERY LAYERS REMOVED
- 3 TBSP WATER
- 6 TBSP OLIVE OIL
- 2 FRESH ROSEMARY SPRIGS
- 1 BAY LEAF
- 7 OZ/200 G SOFT GOAT CHEESE
- 1 TBSP CHOPPED FRESH MIXED HERBS, SUCH AS PARSLEY AND OREGANO
- 1 FRENCH BAGUETTE, SLICED
- SALT AND PEPPER
- SALAD GREENS, TO GARNISH

1 Preheat the oven to 400°F/200°C. Place the garlic in an ovenproof dish. Add the water, half the oil, the rosemary, and bay leaf. Season to taste with salt and pepper. Cover with foil and roast for 30 minutes.

2 Remove the dish from the oven and baste the garlic with the cooking juices. Re-cover and roast for an additional 15 minutes, or until tender.

3 Meanwhile, beat the cheese in a bowl until smooth, then beat in the mixed herbs. Heat the remaining oil in a skillet. Cook the bread on both sides for 3–4 minutes, or until golden brown.

4 Arrange the bread and cheese on serving plates garnished with salad greens. Remove the garlic from the oven. Break up the bulbs but do not peel. Divide between the plates and serve at once. Each diner squeezes the garlic pulp onto the bread and eats it with the cheese.

GARLIC SPAGHETTI

SERVES 4

INGREDIENTS

- ½ CUP OLIVE OIL
- 3 GARLIC CLOVES, CRUSHED
- 1 LB/450 G FRESH SPAGHETTI
- 3 TBSP COARSELY CHOPPED
  FRESH PARSLEY
- SALT AND PEPPER

1 Reserve 1 tablespoon of the olive oil and heat the remainder in a medium saucepan. Add the garlic and a pinch of salt and cook over low heat, stirring constantly, until golden brown, then remove the saucepan from the heat. Do not let the garlic burn because this will taint its flavor. (If it does burn, you will have to start all over again!)

2 Meanwhile, bring a large saucepan of lightly salted water to a boil. Add the spaghetti and remaining olive oil and cook for 2–3 minutes, or until tender but still firm to the bite. Drain the spaghetti thoroughly and return to the saucepan.

3 Add the olive oil and garlic mixture to the spaghetti and toss to coat thoroughly. Season to taste with pepper, then add the chopped fresh parsley and toss to coat again.

4 Transfer the spaghetti to a warm serving dish and serve immediately.

NUTS, SEEDS
& BEANS

Nuts and seeds enable you to incorporate valuable vitamins and "good" fats into your diet on a daily basis. Protein-rich beans are staples of the vegetarian kitchen, but the recipes in this chapter show there is more to the vegetarian diet than nut cutlets! These recipes come from vegetarian cultures around the world and include all-time favorites, such as Hummus, along with the less-familiar Egyptian Brown Beans and the novel Kidney Bean Risotto.

DIRECTORY OF NUTS & SEEDS

Nuts and seeds are more than just a convenient snack—they make a useful and healthy addition to both sweet and savory vegetarian dishes. Best bought in small quantities from stores that have a high turnover of goods, seeds and nuts—particularly if shelled—can go off if kept for too long after purchase. Stored in an airtight container in a cool, dark place, nuts and seeds should last about three months.

Nuts

Nuts are the fruits of trees, with the exception of peanuts, which grow underground. Although fairly high in fat, it is the beneficial omega-6 type, and nuts also provide a range of other nutrients, including protein, the B vitamins, iron, selenium, vitamin E, and zinc. Nuts are available whole, with or without shells, blanched, slivered, chopped, ground, or toasted.

Brazil nuts
Brazil nuts have a sweet, milky taste and are particularly rich in omega-6 essential fatty acids. They are often used in muesli-type breakfast cereals or in desserts.

Macadamia nuts
Macadamia nuts have a creamy, rich, buttery flavor and a high-fat content. The round nut is usually sold shelled, because the outer casing is extremely hard to crack.

Almonds
Almonds come in two types: bitter and sweet. The former is not recommended raw, but is transformed into a fragrant oil and essence. Sweet almonds are best bought shelled in their skins. You can blanch them yourself in boiling water for a few minutes to remove the skin. However, you can also buy them already blanched as well as slivered, toasted, and ground, all of which add a richness and pronounced flavor to cakes, desserts, and some savory dishes.

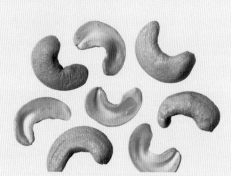

Cashews
Cashews are lower in fat than most other nuts. Their creamy flavor lends itself to roasts, bakes, and nut butters, and they add a pleasant crunch to noodle dishes and salads.

Hazelnuts
The versatile hazelnut is sold whole, shelled, chopped, and ground, and is good roasted. Hazelnuts can be used in both savory and sweet dishes.

Chestnuts
Cooked or roasted chestnuts have a delicious sweet taste and floury texture; they are also really low in fat. They add substance to stuffings, roasts, bakes, and pies. Sweetened chestnut puree is used in desserts.

Pine nuts
The pine nut is one of the key ingredients in pesto and the tiny cream-colored nut has a rich, creamy flavor, which is enhanced by toasting. Buy pine nuts in small quantities because their high-fat content means that they will go off quite quickly.

Walnuts
When picked young, walnuts are referred to as "wet" and have a fresh, milky kernel. However, they are usually bought dried—shelled, chopped, or ground—when the nut adopts a slightly bitter flavor.

Coconut
Coconut is high in saturated fat, so is best eaten in moderation. Coconut milk and cream add a rich creaminess to sauces, curries, smoothies, desserts, and soups. The dense white "meat" is also made into dry unsweetened or flaked coconut.

Seeds

Albeit tiny, seeds pack a powerful punch when it comes to nutritional status. They are a good source of the antioxidant vitamin E, and iron, as well as the essential fatty acid omega-6,

which may help in reducing harmful cholesterol levels—all that from a small and unassuming seed!

Sesame seeds
Tiny sesame seeds come in black or white and are used to make a surprising range of products. Ground into a thick paste, they make tahini, the basis of hummus, and the sweet confection halva; they are also turned into a rich, toasted oil. Their flavor is improved by toasting in a dry skillet until golden. Sprinkle over salads, noodles, bakes, cakes, and breads.

Sunflower seeds
Toasting also improves the flavor of sunflower seeds, but be careful not to burn them or their nutritional content will be affected. The tear-shaped seeds have similar uses to sesame seeds and make a healthy addition to salads, breakfast cereals, and granola bars.

Pumpkin seeds
Pumpkin seeds are one of the few plant foods to contain both omega-3 and omega-6 essential fatty acids and

are richer in iron than other seeds. They make a nutritious snack or can be used in much the same way as other seeds.

Poppy seeds
These small black seeds add an attractive decorative look as well as crunch to breads and cakes. They are used in German and Eastern European pastries, strudels, and tarts.

Linseeds
Long known for their oil, used to polish wood, these small, golden seeds are also known as flax seeds. Linseeds are one of the few vegetarian sources of omega-3 essential fatty acids and can be sprinkled over breakfast cereals and salads or mixed into breads and pastries.

How to Toast Nuts and Seeds

To remove the papery husk from hazelnuts or almonds, simply put the nuts on a baking sheet and heat in a preheated oven at 350°F/180°C for 5–10 minutes to loosen the skins. Remove from the oven and, when they are cool enough to handle, rub off the skins with a clean dish towel.

Seeds and nuts, such as whole or slivered almonds, are also toasted to enhance their flavor. Smaller quantities of seeds can be toasted in a dry skillet until they change color, but for larger amounts, spread them in a single layer on a baking sheet and roast in a preheated oven at 350°F/180°C for 5–7 minutes.

DIRECTORY OF BEANS

Lentils, beans, and peas are an excellent source of lowfat protein as well as complex carbohydrates, vitamins, minerals, and fiber. Their versatility and ability to absorb the flavors of other foods mean that they can form the basis of a large number of different and satisfying dishes.

Although beans can be kept for up to a year, they tend to toughen with age. Buy them from stores with a high turnover of stock and look for bright, unwrinkled beans that are not dusty. Store beans in an airtight container in a cool, dark place and rinse them before use. Avoid adding salt to the water when cooking beans because this prevents them from softening; instead, season them when cooked.

Lentils
Unlike most other beans, lentils do not require presoaking and are relatively quick to cook. They are sold dried or canned and can be used in a variety of dishes—dals, burgers, bakes, stews, and soups.

Split lentils
Orange-colored red lentils are the most familiar variety and, because they are "split," they can be cooked in around 20 minutes, eventually disintegrating into a thick puree. They are ideal for thickening soups and stews, and are used to make the spicy Indian dish known as dal.

Brown lentils
These disk-shaped lentils, sometimes called Continental lentils, have a robust texture and flavor. Available whole, they take longer to cook than red lentils—around 45 minutes—and add substance to stews, stuffings, and soups.

Green lentils
Similar to the brown lentil, green lentils have a slightly milder flavor and can be cooked and blended with herbs and garlic to make a nutritious spread. The tiny, dark gray-green Puy lentil is grown in France and is considered superior in flavor to other varieties. They take around 25–30 minutes to cook, but retain their beadlike shape. They are deli-

cious in warm salads with a vinai-grette dressing and also make a hearty addition to stews.

Dried peas
Unlike lentils, peas are soft when young and need to be dried. Available whole or split, the latter have a sweeter flavor and cook more quickly.

Yellow and green split peas
Yellow and green split peas are interchangeable with red split lentils and are perfect for dals, soups, casseroles, and purees, but they do take slightly longer to cook.

NUTS, SEEDS & BEANS 153

Beans

With the exception of the ubiquitous baked bean, beans are often ignored, yet they are all so versatile, lending themselves to inclusion in pies, bakes, stews, soups, pâtés, dips, burgers, salads, and more. What often puts people off is the long soaking time, but canned beans are just as good and incredibly convenient. Just drain and rinse before use.

Chickpeas

Chickpeas resemble shelled hazelnuts and have a nutty flavor and a creamy texture. They are widely used in Indian and Middle-Eastern cuisines. In India, they are ground to make the yellow-colored chickpea flour, which is used for making fritters and flatbreads.

Flageolet and borlotti

The pretty, pale-green flageolet bean has a fresh, delicate taste and soft texture, while the hearty borlotti bean is pinkish brown in color with a sweetish flavor and tender texture, and is often used to make Italian bean and pasta soups.

Cannellini

These white, kidney-shaped beans have a soft, creamy texture when cooked. They are equally delicious served warm in salads or pureed to make a tasty, nutritious alternative to mashed potatoes.

Red kidney

Red kidney beans have a soft, "starchy" texture and retain their color and shape when cooked. They are used to make Mexican refried beans and are essential to a successful chili.

Navy and great Northern

Navy and great Northern beans are most commonly used for canned baked beans, but the ivory-colored beans are also good in stews and soups.

Lima

Lima beans are similar in flavor and appearance to navy and great Northern beans. These cream-colored, kidney-shaped beans have a soft, starchy texture.

Soy

This versatile bean has all the nutritional properties of animal products, but none of the disadvantages. Soybeans range in color from creamy yellow through brown-black and make a healthy addition to soups, casseroles, and bakes. The dried beans are very dense and need to be soaked for 12 hours before cooking. Soybeans are used to make tofu, tempeh, textured soy protein (ground meat replacement and chunks), flour, soy milk, soy sauce, and miso, as well as a range of sauces, including black bean sauce, yellow bean sauce, and Peking sauce.

Cooking Beans

Once soaked, beans should be drained and rinsed in clean water. Any beans that have floated to the surface during soaking should be discarded. You need to use plenty of water for cooking: 5 cups/ 1.2 liters fresh cold water per 1 lb/450 g beans. Bring to a boil over high heat and boil for 10 minutes, then reduce the heat and simmer until the beans are soft but not mushy, which can take anywhere from 30 minutes to 2 hours, depending on the type and age of the bean. The beans must always be submerged; add more boiling water as necessary to keep them covered by about ½ inch/1 cm. The cooking water can be used as a vegetable stock. If you are cooking more than one variety of bean, they need to be soaked and cooked separately, because they will cook at different rates. Remember to add salt only toward the end of cooking.

CHILLED PEA SOUP

SERVES 3–4

INGREDIENTS

- SCANT 2 CUPS VEGETABLE STOCK OR WATER
- 4 CUPS FROZEN PEAS
- 4 SCALLIONS
- 1¼ CUPS PLAIN YOGURT OR LIGHT CREAM
- SALT AND PEPPER

TO GARNISH

- 2 TBSP CHOPPED FRESH MINT, SCALLIONS, OR CHIVES
- GRATED LEMON ZEST

1 Bring the stock to a boil in a large saucepan over medium heat. Reduce the heat, add the peas and scallions, and simmer for 5 minutes.

2 Cool slightly, then strain twice, making sure that you remove any pieces of skin. Pour into a large bowl, season to taste, and stir in the yogurt or cream. Cover the bowl with plastic wrap and chill for several hours in the refrigerator.

3 To serve, remove from the refrigerator, mix well, and ladle into a large tureen or individual soup bowls or mugs. Garnish with chopped mint, scallions, or chives, and grated lemon zest.

CHICKPEA SOUP

SERVES 6

INGREDIENTS

- GENEROUS 2¼ CUPS DRIED CHICKPEAS, SOAKED IN COLD WATER OVERNIGHT
- 2 TBSP OLIVE OIL
- 1 ONION, FINELY CHOPPED
- 2 GARLIC CLOVES, FINELY CHOPPED
- 1 LB/450 G SWISS CHARD, TRIMMED AND FINELY SLICED
- 2 FRESH ROSEMARY SPRIGS
- 14 OZ/400 G CANNED CHOPPED TOMATOES
- SALT AND PEPPER
- SLICES OF TOASTED BREAD, TO SERVE

1 Drain the chickpeas and put in a large saucepan. Cover with fresh cold water and bring to a boil, using a slotted spoon to skim off any foam that rises to the surface. Reduce the heat and simmer, uncovered, for 1–1¼ hours, or until tender, adding more water if necessary.

2 Drain the chickpeas, reserving the cooking water. Season the chickpeas well with salt and pepper. Put two-thirds in a food processor or blender with some of the reserved cooking water and process until smooth, adding more of the cooking water if necessary to give a thinner consistency. Return to the saucepan.

3 Heat the oil in a medium saucepan, then add the onion and garlic and cook over medium heat, stirring frequently, for 3–4 minutes, or until the onion has softened. Add the Swiss chard and rosemary sprigs and cook, stirring frequently, for 3–4 minutes. Add the tomatoes and cook for an additional 5 minutes, or until the tomatoes have broken down to an almost smooth sauce. Remove the rosemary sprigs.

4 Add the Swiss chard and tomato mixture to the chickpea puree and simmer for 2–3 minutes. Taste and adjust the seasoning if necessary.

5 Serve in warmed bowls with warm slices of toasted bread on the side.

HUMMUS TOASTS WITH OLIVES

SERVES 4

INGREDIENTS

- 1½ CUPS CANNED CHICKPEAS
- JUICE OF 1 LARGE LEMON
- 6 TBSP SESAME SEED PASTE (TAHINI)
- 2 TBSP OLIVE OIL
- 2 GARLIC CLOVES, FINELY CHOPPED
- SALT AND PEPPER
- CHOPPED FRESH CILANTRO AND BLACK OLIVES, TO GARNISH

TOASTS

- 1 CIABATTA LOAF, SLICED
- 2 GARLIC CLOVES, FINELY CHOPPED
- 1 TBSP CHOPPED FRESH CILANTRO
- 4 TBSP OLIVE OIL

1 To make the hummus, first drain the chickpeas, reserving a little of the liquid. Put the chickpeas and liquid in a food processor and blend, gradually adding the reserved liquid and lemon juice. Blend well after each addition until smooth.

2 Stir in the sesame seed paste and all but 1 teaspoon of the olive oil. Add the garlic, season to taste, and blend again until smooth.

3 Spoon the hummus into a serving dish. Drizzle the remaining olive oil over the top, and garnish with chopped cilantro and olives. Cover and chill in the refrigerator while preparing the toasts.

4 Lay the slices of ciabatta on a broiler rack in a single layer.

5 Mix the garlic, cilantro, and olive oil together and drizzle over the bread slices. Cook under a hot broiler for 2–3 minutes, until golden brown, turning once. Serve hot with the hummus.

KE OBANA
y.daisuke@misterhollywood.jp
101 TOKYO JAPAN
'.0978
KU OSAKA-SHI 550.0013 OSAKA JAPAN
1705

CHICKPEA & VEGETABLE STEW

SERVES 4

INGREDIENTS

- 8 OZ/225 G DRIED CHICKPEAS, SOAKED IN COLD WATER OVERNIGHT
- 3 TBSP OLIVE OIL
- 1 LARGE ONION, SLICED
- 2 GARLIC CLOVES, FINELY CHOPPED
- 2 LEEKS, SLICED
- 6 OZ/175 G CARROTS, SLICED
- 4 TURNIPS, SLICED
- 4 CELERY STALKS, SLICED
- ⅔ CUP BULGUR WHEAT
- 14 OZ/400 G CANNED CHOPPED TOMATOES
- 2 TBSP SNIPPED FRESH CHIVES, PLUS EXTRA TO GARNISH
- SALT AND PEPPER

1 Drain the chickpeas and place in a heavy saucepan. Add enough water to cover, bring to a boil, and simmer for $1\frac{1}{2}$ hours.

2 Meanwhile, heat the oil in a large saucepan. Add the onion and cook, stirring occasionally, for 5 minutes, until soft. Add the garlic, leeks, carrots, turnips, and celery and cook, stirring occasionally, for 5 minutes.

3 Stir in the bulgur, tomatoes, and chives, season to taste with salt and pepper, and bring to a boil. Spoon the mixture into a heatproof bowl and cover with a lid or circle of foil.

4 When the chickpeas have been cooking for $1\frac{1}{2}$ hours, set a steamer over the saucepan. Place the bowl of vegetables in the steamer, cover tightly, and cook for 40 minutes. Remove the bowl from the steamer, drain the chickpeas, then stir them into the vegetable and bulgur mixture. Transfer the stew to a warm serving dish and serve immediately, garnished with the extra chives.

VEGETABLE & BLACK
BEAN SPRING ROLLS

SERVES 4

INGREDIENTS

- 2 TBSP PEANUT OIL OR VEGETABLE OIL, PLUS EXTRA FOR DEEP-FRYING
- 4 SCALLIONS, CUT INTO 2-INCH/5-CM LENGTHS AND SHREDDED LENGTHWISE, PLUS EXTRA TO GARNISH
- 1-INCH/2.5-CM PIECE FRESH GINGER, PEELED AND FINELY CHOPPED
- 1 LARGE CARROT, PEELED AND CUT INTO THIN STICKS
- 1 RED BELL PEPPER, SEEDED AND CUT INTO THIN STICKS
- 6 TBSP BLACK BEAN SAUCE
- ⅓ CUP FRESH BEAN SPROUTS
- 7 OZ/200 G CANNED WATER CHESTNUTS, DRAINED AND COARSELY CHOPPED
- 2-INCH/5-CM PIECE CUCUMBER, CUT INTO THIN STICKS
- EIGHT 8-INCH/20-CM SQUARE EGG ROLL SKINS
- SWEET CHILI DIPPING SAUCE, TO SERVE (OPTIONAL)

1 Heat the oil in a preheated wok. Add the scallions, ginger, carrot, and red bell pepper, then stir-fry over medium-high heat for 2–3 minutes. Add the black bean sauce, bean sprouts, water chestnuts, and cucumber and stir-fry for 1–2 minutes. Remove from the heat and cool.

2 Remove the egg roll skins from the package, but keep them in a pile and covered with plastic wrap to prevent them from drying out. Lay one skin in a diamond shape on a counter in front of you and brush the edges with water. Put a spoonful of the filling near one corner and fold the corner over the filling. Roll over again and then fold the side corners over the filling. Roll up to seal the filling completely. Repeat with the remaining skins and filling.

3 Heat the oil for deep-frying in a wok, deep saucepan, or deep-fat fryer to 350–375°F/180–190°C, or until a cube of bread browns in 30 seconds. Add the rolls in 2–3 batches, and cook for 2–3 minutes, or until crisp and golden all over. Remove with a slotted spoon and drain on paper towels, then keep warm while you cook the remaining rolls. Garnish with shredded scallions, and serve with sweet chili dipping sauce if using.

BEAN BURGERS

MAKES 4

INGREDIENTS

- 1 TBSP SUNFLOWER OIL, PLUS EXTRA FOR BRUSHING
- 1 ONION, FINELY CHOPPED
- 1 GARLIC CLOVE, FINELY CHOPPED
- 1 TSP GROUND CORIANDER
- 1 TSP GROUND CUMIN
- 4 OZ/115 G WHITE MUSHROOMS, FINELY CHOPPED
- 15 OZ/425 G CANNED PINTO OR RED KIDNEY BEANS, DRAINED AND RINSED
- 2 TBSP CHOPPED FRESH FLAT-LEAF PARSLEY
- ALL-PURPOSE FLOUR, FOR DUSTING
- SALT AND PEPPER
- HAMBURGER BUNS, AND SALAD, TO SERVE

1 Heat the oil in a heavy-bottom skillet over medium heat. Add the onion and cook, stirring frequently, for 5 minutes, or until softened. Add the garlic, coriander, and cumin and cook, stirring, for an additional minute. Add the mushrooms and cook, stirring frequently, for 4–5 minutes, until all the liquid has evaporated. Transfer to a bowl.

2 Put the beans in a small bowl and mash with a fork. Stir into the mushroom mixture with the parsley and season to taste with salt and pepper.

3 Preheat the broiler to medium–high. Divide the mixture equally into 4 portions, dust lightly with flour, and shape into flat, round burgers. Brush with oil and cook under the broiler for 4–5 minutes on each side. Serve in hamburger buns with salad.

FAVA BEANS WITH FETA

SERVES 4–6

INGREDIENTS

- 1 LB 2 OZ/500 G SHELLED FAVA BEANS
- 4 TBSP EXTRA VIRGIN OLIVE OIL
- 1 TBSP LEMON JUICE
- 1 TBSP FINELY CHOPPED FRESH DILL, PLUS EXTRA TO GARNISH
- 2 OZ/55 G FETA CHEESE, DRAINED AND DICED
- SALT AND PEPPER

1 Bring a saucepan of water to a boil. Add the fava beans and cook for about 2 minutes, until tender. Drain thoroughly and set aside.

2 When the beans are cool enough to handle, remove and discard the outer skins to reveal the bright green beans underneath. Put the peeled beans in a serving bowl.

3 Combine the olive oil and lemon juice, then season to taste with salt and pepper. Pour the dressing over the warm beans, add the dill, and stir gently. Adjust the seasoning, if necessary.

4 If serving hot, add the feta cheese, toss gently, and sprinkle with extra dill, then serve immediately. Alternatively, set aside the beans in their dressing to cool and then chill until required.

5 To serve cold, remove from the refrigerator 10 minutes before serving to bring to room temperature. Taste and adjust the seasoning, if necessary, then sprinkle with the feta and extra dill.

SAUCY BORLOTTI BEANS

SERVES 4–6

INGREDIENTS

- 1 LB 5 OZ/600 G FRESH BORLOTTI BEANS
- 4 LARGE LEAVES FRESH SAGE, TORN
- 1 TBSP OLIVE OIL
- 1 LARGE ONION, THINLY SLICED
- 1¼ CUPS GOOD-QUALITY BOTTLED OR HOMEMADE TOMATO SAUCE (SEE PAGE 37) FOR PASTA
- SALT AND PEPPER
- FRESH SAGE LEAVES, TO GARNISH

1 Shell the borlotti beans. Bring a saucepan of water to a boil, add the beans and torn sage leaves, bring back to a boil, and simmer for about 12 minutes, or until tender. Drain and set aside.

2 Heat the olive oil in a large, heavy skillet over medium heat. Add the onion and cook, stirring occasionally, for about 5 minutes, until softened and translucent but not browned. Stir the tomato sauce into the skillet with the cooked borlotti beans and the fresh sage leaves.

3 Increase the heat and bring to a boil, stirring. Lower the heat, partially cover, and simmer for about 10 minutes, or until the sauce has slightly reduced.

4 Adjust the seasoning, transfer to a serving bowl, and serve hot, garnished with fresh sage leaves.

INGREDIENTS

- 1³/₄ CUPS DRIED FAVA BEANS,
  RINSED AND SOAKED IN COLD
  WATER FOR AT LEAST 12 HOURS
  WITH 1 TBSP BAKING SODA
- 2 TBSP OLIVE OIL
- 1 ONION, FINELY CHOPPED
- 1 LARGE GARLIC CLOVE,
  CRUSHED TO A PASTE WITH
  1 TSP SALT
- 1 LARGE TOMATO, SEEDED AND
  FINELY CHOPPED
- SALT AND PEPPER

TO SERVE

- 1 FRESH RED CHILE, SEEDED
  OR UNSEEDED TO TASTE AND
  FINELY CHOPPED, OR ¹/₂ TSP
  DRIED CHILE FLAKES (OPTIONAL)
- 1 LEMON, HALVED
- EXTRA VIRGIN OLIVE OIL
- WARMED ARAB FLATBREAD
  OR PITAS

EGYPTIAN
BROWN BEANS

1 Drain the beans and rinse well. Put them in a saucepan with fresh cold water to cover and bring to a boil. Boil rapidly for 10 minutes, skimming off any foam that rises to the surface. Reduce the heat to low, cover, and simmer for at least 2 hours, or until tender enough to be easily mashed between your fingers, adding more water as necessary. The exact simmering time will depend on how old the beans are—the older they are, the longer they will take. Drain the beans, reserving the cooking water. At this point, chefs and perfectionists insist that the beans should be peeled, but most home cooks don't bother—the choice is yours.

2 Heat the olive oil in a large skillet. Add the onion and cook over medium heat, stirring frequently, for 3 minutes. Add the crushed garlic and cook, stirring frequently, for an additional 2 minutes, or until the onion is very soft and golden but not brown. Use a slotted spoon to transfer half the beans to the skillet, stir, and mash into the onion. Add the remaining beans and tomato and heat through. Add salt and pepper to taste. If the mixture is too thick to be scooped up with flatbread, slowly add some of the reserved cooking water until you reach the desired consistency.

3 Spoon the beans into a serving bowl. Sprinkle the chile over the top, if using, then squeeze over juice from the lemon halves to taste and drizzle with extra virgin olive oil. Serve with warmed Arab flatbread or pitas for scooping up the beans.

GREEN BEAN SALAD
WITH FETA

SERVES 4

INGREDIENTS

- 12 OZ/350 G GREEN BEANS, TRIMMED
- 1 RED ONION, CHOPPED
- 3–4 TBSP CHOPPED FRESH CILANTRO
- 2 RADISHES, THINLY SLICED
- ¾ CUP CRUMBLED FETA CHEESE
- 1 TSP CHOPPED FRESH OREGANO OR ½ TSP DRIED OREGANO
- 2 TBSP RED WINE VINEGAR OR FRUIT VINEGAR
- 5 TBSP EXTRA VIRGIN OLIVE OIL
- 3 RIPE TOMATOES (OPTIONAL), CUT INTO WEDGES
- PEPPER

1 Bring about 2 inches/5 cm water to a boil in the bottom of a steamer or in a medium saucepan. Add the green beans to the top of the steamer or place them in a metal colander set over the saucepan of water. Cover and steam the beans for about 5 minutes, until just tender.

2 Transfer the beans to a bowl and add the onion, cilantro, radishes, crumbled feta cheese, and oregano.

3 Grind pepper over to taste. Whisk the vinegar and olive oil together and then pour over the salad. Toss gently to mix well.

4 Transfer to a serving platter, surround with the tomato wedges if using, and serve at once or chill until ready to serve.

SESAME HOT
NOODLES

SERVES 4

INGREDIENTS
- 1 LB 2 OZ/500 G DRIED MEDIUM
  EGG NOODLES
- 3 TBSP SUNFLOWER OIL
- 2 TBSP SESAME OIL
- 1 GARLIC CLOVE, CRUSHED
- 1 TBSP SMOOTH PEANUT
  BUTTER
- 1 SMALL GREEN CHILE, SEEDED
  AND VERY FINELY CHOPPED
- 3 TBSP TOASTED SESAME SEEDS
- 4 TBSP LIGHT SOY SAUCE
- ½ TBSP LIME JUICE
- SALT AND PEPPER
- 4 TBSP CHOPPED FRESH
  CILANTRO

1 Place the noodles in a large saucepan of boiling water, then immediately remove from the heat. Cover and let the noodles stand for 6 minutes, stirring once halfway through the time. At the end of 6 minutes the noodles will be perfectly cooked. Alternatively, cook the noodles following the package instructions.

2 Meanwhile, make the dressing. Mix together the sunflower oil, sesame oil, crushed garlic, and peanut butter in a mixing bowl until smooth.

3 Add the chopped green chile, sesame seeds, and light soy sauce to the other dressing ingredients. Add the lime juice, according to taste, and mix well. Season with salt and pepper. Drain the noodles thoroughly, then place in a warmed serving bowl.

4 Add the dressing and chopped fresh cilantro to the noodles and toss well to mix. Serve hot as a main course or as an accompaniment.

PASTA WITH PESTO

SERVES 4

INGREDIENTS
- 1 LB/450 G DRIED TAGLIATELLE
- SALT
- FRESH BASIL SPRIGS, TO GARNISH

PESTO
- 2 GARLIC CLOVES
- ¼ CUP PINE NUTS
- 2½ CUPS FRESH BASIL LEAVES
- ½ CUP FRESHLY GRATED PARMESAN CHEESE
- ½ CUP OLIVE OIL
- SALT

1 To make the pesto, put the garlic, pine nuts, a large pinch of salt, and the basil into a mortar, and pound to a paste with a pestle. Transfer to a bowl and gradually work in the Parmesan cheese with a wooden spoon, followed by the olive oil, to make a thick, creamy sauce. Taste and adjust the seasoning if necessary.

2 Alternatively, put the garlic, pine nuts, and a large pinch of salt into a food processor or blender and process briefly. Add the basil leaves and process to a paste. With the motor still running, gradually add the olive oil. Scrape into a bowl and beat in the Parmesan cheese. Season to taste with salt.

3 Bring a large saucepan of lightly salted water to a boil. Add the pasta, return to a boil, and cook for 8–10 minutes, or until tender but still firm to the bite. Drain the pasta well, return to the saucepan, and toss with half the pesto, then divide among warmed serving plates and top with the remaining pesto. Garnish with basil sprigs and serve immediately.

NUTTY BLEU CHEESE ROAST

SERVES 6–8

INGREDIENTS

- 2 TBSP VIRGIN OLIVE OIL, PLUS EXTRA FOR OILING
- 2 ONIONS
- 3–5 GARLIC CLOVES, CRUSHED
- 2 CELERY STALKS, FINELY SLICED
- 6 OZ/175 G COOKED AND PEELED CHESTNUTS
- GENEROUS 1 CUP MIXED CHOPPED NUTS
- SCANT ⅔ CUP GROUND ALMONDS
- 1 CUP FRESH WHOLE WHEAT BREADCRUMBS
- 8 OZ/225 G BLEU CHEESE, CRUMBLED
- 1 TBSP CHOPPED FRESH BASIL, PLUS EXTRA SPRIGS TO GARNISH
- 1 EGG, BEATEN
- 1 RED BELL PEPPER, PEELED, SEEDED, AND CUT INTO THIN WEDGES
- 1 ZUCCHINI, ABOUT 4 OZ/115 G, CUT INTO WEDGES
- TOMATO SAUCE (SEE PAGE 37)
- SALT AND PEPPER
- CHERRY TOMATOES, TO GARNISH

1 Preheat the oven to 350°F/180°C. Lightly oil a 9 x 5 x 3-inch/23 x 13 x 8-cm loaf pan.

2 Finely chop one of the onions. Heat half the oil in a skillet and cook the chopped onion, 1–2 of the garlic cloves, and the celery, stirring frequently, for 5 minutes.

3 Remove from the skillet and drain through a colander. Transfer to a food processor with the nuts, breadcrumbs, half the cheese, and the basil. Pulse until blended, then pulse again to blend in the egg to form a stiff mixture. Season to taste with salt and pepper.

4 Cut the remaining onion into thin wedges. Heat the remaining oil in the skillet and cook the onion wedges, remaining garlic, red bell pepper, and zucchini, stirring frequently, for 5 minutes. Remove from the pan, then drain through a colander and add salt and pepper to taste.

5 Place half the nut mixture in the prepared pan and smooth the surface. Arrange the onion and bell pepper mixture on top and crumble over the remaining cheese. Top with the remaining nut mixture and press down. Cover with foil.

6 Bake in the preheated oven for 45 minutes. Remove the foil and bake for an additional 25–35 minutes, or until firm to the touch.

7 Cool for 5 minutes before inverting onto a warmed serving platter. Serve with a little tomato sauce drizzled over the top, garnished with basil sprigs and cherry tomatoes, and accompanied by a salad.

CASHEW PAELLA

SERVES 4

INGREDIENTS

- 1 TBSP BUTTER
- 2 TBSP OLIVE OIL
- 1 RED ONION, CHOPPED
- ¾ CUP MEDIUM-GRAIN PAELLA RICE
- 1 TSP TURMERIC
- 1 TSP GROUND CUMIN
- ½ TSP CHILI POWDER
- 3 GARLIC CLOVES, CRUSHED
- 1 FRESH GREEN CHILE, SLICED
- 1 GREEN BELL PEPPER, SEEDED AND DICED
- 1 RED BELL PEPPER, SEEDED AND DICED
- 16 BABY CORN, HALVED LENGTHWISE
- 2 TBSP PITTED BLACK OLIVES
- 1 LARGE TOMATO, SEEDED AND DICED
- 2 CUPS VEGETABLE STOCK
- GENEROUS ½ CUP UNSALTED CASHEWS
- SCANT ½ CUP FROZEN PEAS
- 2 TBSP CHOPPED FRESH PARSLEY, PLUS EXTRA SPRIGS TO GARNISH
- PINCH OF CAYENNE PEPPER
- SALT AND PEPPER

1 Melt the butter with the oil in a paella pan or wide, shallow skillet and cook the onion over medium heat, stirring, for 2–3 minutes, or until softened.

2 Add the rice, turmeric, cumin, chili powder, garlic, chile, bell peppers, baby corn, olives, and tomato and cook, stirring constantly, for 1–2 minutes. Pour in the stock and bring to a boil. Reduce the heat and cook, stirring frequently, for 20 minutes.

3 Add the nuts and peas and cook, stirring occasionally, for 5 minutes. Season to taste with salt and pepper and sprinkle with the chopped parsley and cayenne pepper. Transfer to warmed serving plates, then garnish with parsley sprigs and serve immediately.

5

BRASSICAS &
LEAVES

There isn't any need to forego the pleasures of eating salads in the winter just because soft, delicate leaves don't appeal at that time of year. This chapter has plenty of ideas for delicious salads that hit the spot all year round and recipes for baking, pureeing, and stir-frying members of the often-neglected cabbage family into dishes family and friends will enjoy. Be sure to make enough for seconds all around!

DIRECTORY OF BRASSICAS & LEAVES

This large group of vegetables includes many old familiars, such as cauliflower, cabbage, and broccoli, as well as more exotic examples, such as bok choy. In the past, these vegetables suffered greatly from overcooking and their associations with institutional cooking, but, properly cooked, they are delicious and have enormous nutritional value.

Brassicas

This large and varied group of vegetables boasts an extraordinary range of health properties and should form a regular part of our diet—at least 3–4 times a week. They provide numerous phytochemicals, a group of compounds that have been found to provide an anticarcinogenic cocktail and play a crucial role in fighting disease by stimulating the body's defences. Brassicas are best cooked lightly. Overcooking them not only destroys many of the nutrients, but also affects their flavor. For this reason, steaming or stir-frying are preferable to boiling. Some people dislike brassicas because of their slight bitterness, so serving them in a cream or cheese sauce may help. They also work well in Asian dishes.

Broccoli

There are two types of broccoli. The slender-stemmed purple sprouting type is the original type of broccoli, with long stalks and small purple flower heads; the leaves, stalks, and head are all edible. The readily available calabrese has a tightly budded top and thick stalk. Choose broccoli with dark green or purple florets and avoid any with signs of yellowing or a wilted stalk. When serving broccoli, do not forget the stalk, which is also nutritious. The stalk can be served raw, grated into salads, or cut into crudités.

Cabbage

When lightly cooked or served shredded in a salad, cabbage is delicious. Cabbages range from the crinkly-leaved Savoy, which is ideal for stuffing, to the smooth and firm white and red varieties. Add a little vinegar to the cooking water when

preparing red cabbage to preserve its color. Chinese cabbage has a more delicate flavor and is good in salads or stir-fries.

Cauliflower

Cauliflower comes in many varieties, ranging from white to pale green and purple, but all should be encased in green outer leaves because these protect the more delicate florets.

Brussels sprouts

Reminiscent of Christmas, Brussels sprouts are like miniature cabbages and have a strong, nutty flavor. Sprouts are sweeter when picked after the first frost. They are best cooked very lightly or, better still, stir-fried.

Chard
Like spinach, chard should have dark green leaves and a white or red stem. Since the stem takes longer to cook than the leaves, it is best sliced and cooked slightly before the leaves are added. Spinach beet is similar to Swiss chard and has a mild flavor. Spring greens are full of flavor and nutrients and should have dark green leaves.

Bok choy
The most typical bok choy features dark green leaves at the top of thick, white, upright stalks. It has a mild flavor, which makes it popular with children, and makes a delightful addition to stir-fries, soups, noodle dishes, and salads. The stalk takes slightly longer to cook than the leaves.

Salad greens
Salad greens come in a huge variety of shapes, textures, colors, and flavors, from the bitter-tasting endive to peppery watercress and delicate butterhead lettuce. Convenient bags of mixed salad greens enable you to sample a wide range of different types, although they do not tend to last as long as the individually packed types.

Lettuce
Romaine and Iceberg have firm, crisp leaves, while Boston is a smaller, sweeter version of romaine. The pretty frilly leaves of red leaf are green at the bottom and a deep red around the edge. Equally attractive is the oakleaf lettuce. Nutritionally, lettuce is best eaten raw, with the darker outer leaves containing more nutrients than the pale-colored inner leaves. However, it can also be braised, steamed, and turned into soups.

Other salad leaves
Cress, mizuna, arugula, and watercress have a strong, distinctive flavor and will enliven any salad. Escarole, frisée, and radicchio are slightly bitter in flavor and are best used in moderation because they can easily dominate a salad.

Leafy greens
Research into the health benefits of leafy greens shows that by eating spinach, chard, bok choy, spring greens, and spinach beet on a regular basis, you may protect yourself against certain forms of cancer. Leafy vegetables are tastiest served steamed or stir-fried and go particularly well with Asian dishes that include garlic, ginger, chile, and soy sauce.

Spinach
Spinach does provide iron, but not in such rich amounts as was once believed and in a form that is not easy to assimilate. However, combining spinach with vitamin C-rich foods increases absorption. Nutritionally, it is most beneficial when eaten raw and the young leaves are best for this.

BROCCOLI & CHEESE SOUP

SERVES 6

INGREDIENTS

- 2 TBSP BUTTER
- 1 ONION, CHOPPED
- 1 LB/450 G POTATOES, PEELED AND GRATED
- 2 FRESH TARRAGON LEAVES
- 3 PINTS/1.7 LITERS VEGETABLE STOCK
- 1 LB 8 OZ/675 G BROCCOLI, CUT INTO SMALL FLORETS
- 6 OZ/175 G CHEDDAR CHEESE
- 1 TBSP CHOPPED FRESH PARSLEY
- SALT AND GROUND BLACK PEPPER

1 Melt the butter in a large, heavy saucepan. Add the onion and cook, stirring occasionally, for 5 minutes, until soft. Add the grated potatoes and tarragon, season to taste with salt and pepper, and mix well. Pour in just enough of the stock to cover and bring to a boil. Lower the heat, cover, and simmer for 10 minutes.

2 Meanwhile, bring the remaining stock to a boil in another saucepan. Add the broccoli and cook for 6-8 minutes, until just tender.

3 Remove both pans from the heat, cool slightly, then ladle the contents of both pans into a blender or food processor. Process until smooth, then pour the mixture into a clean saucepan. Grate in the cheese, add the parsley, and heat gently to warm through, but do not let the soup boil. Ladle into warmed soup bowls and serve immediately.

TRADITIONAL BEAN & CABBAGE SOUP

SERVES 6

INGREDIENTS

- SCANT 1¼ CUPS DRIED CANNELLINI BEANS, SOAKED IN COLD WATER OVERNIGHT
- 3 TBSP OLIVE OIL
- 2 RED ONIONS, COARSELY CHOPPED
- 4 CARROTS, PEELED AND SLICED
- 4 CELERY STALKS, COARSELY CHOPPED
- 4 GARLIC CLOVES, COARSELY CHOPPED
- 2½ CUPS WATER OR VEGETABLE STOCK
- 14 OZ/400 G CANNED CHOPPED TOMATOES
- 2 TBSP CHOPPED FRESH FLAT-LEAF PARSLEY
- 1 LB 2 OZ/500 G CAVOLO NERO ("BLACK" CABBAGE), OR GREEN CABBAGE IF UNAVAILABLE, TRIMMED AND FINELY SLICED
- 1 SMALL 2-DAY-OLD CIABATTA LOAF, TORN INTO SMALL PIECES
- SALT AND PEPPER
- EXTRA VIRGIN OLIVE OIL, TO SERVE

1 Drain the beans and put in a large saucepan. Cover with fresh cold water and bring to a boil, using a slotted spoon to skim off any foam that rises to the surface. Reduce the heat and simmer, uncovered, for 1–1½ hours, or until tender, topping off with water if required.

2 Meanwhile, heat the olive oil in a large saucepan, then add the onions, carrots, and celery and cook over medium heat, stirring frequently, for 10–15 minutes, or until softened. Add the garlic and cook, stirring, for 1–2 minutes.

3 Drain the beans, reserving the cooking water, and add half the beans to the vegetable mixture. Pour in the measured water and the tomatoes, then add the parsley and season well with salt and pepper. Bring to a simmer and cook, uncovered and stirring occasionally, for 30 minutes. Add the cavolo nero and cook, stirring occasionally, for an additional 15 minutes.

4 Put the remaining beans in a food processor or blender with some of the reserved cooking water and process until smooth. Add to the soup. Stir in the bread. The soup should be thick, but add more of the reserved cooking water to thin if necessary. Continue to cook until heated through.

5 Serve hot with a drizzle of extra virgin olive oil.

SPINACH & FETA TRIANGLES

MAKES 12

INGREDIENTS

- 12 SHEETS FILO PIE DOUGH, ABOUT 12 X 9 INCHES/30 X 23 CM EACH, THAWED IF FROZEN
- 1 CUP UNSALTED BUTTER, MELTED AND COOLED

FILLING

- 9 OZ/250 G BABY SPINACH LEAVES, ANY THICK STEMS REMOVED, RINSED, AND SHAKEN DRY
- 2 TBSP OLIVE OIL, PLUS EXTRA FOR OILING
- 4 SCALLIONS, FINELY CHOPPED
- 1 SMALL GARLIC CLOVE, CRUSHED
- 2 TBSP CHOPPED FRESH DILL
- 4½ OZ/125 G GREEK FETA CHEESE (DRAINED WEIGHT), CRUMBLED
- 1 LARGE EGG, BEATEN
- ¼ TSP FRESHLY GRATED NUTMEG
- 2 TBSP PINE NUTS, TOASTED (OPTIONAL)
- 2 TBSP RAISINS (OPTIONAL)
- SALT (OPTIONAL) AND PEPPER

1 For the filling, put the spinach, with only the water clinging to its leaves, in a large saucepan, cover, and cook over medium heat, stirring occasionally, for 10 minutes, or until tender. Drain and cool. Squeeze out all excess moisture, put in a large mixing bowl, and set aside.

2 Heat the oil in a skillet. Add the scallions and cook over medium heat, stirring, for 1 minute. Add the garlic and cook, stirring, for 1–2 minutes, then add to the bowl with the remaining ingredients, raisins if using, and pepper to taste—it will be runny. Cook a small amount in the skillet to see if it needs salt, but the salt in the feta should suffice.

3 Preheat the oven to 375°F/190°C. Brush 1 or 2 baking sheets with oil. Lay a filo sheet on a counter and brush with melted butter. Top with another sheet, brush with butter, then add a third and brush with butter. Cut them into long strips 3 inches/7.5 cm wide. Cut a total of 12 sets of strips. Arrange one set vertically in front of you. Cover the filo you are not using with damp (not wet) paper towels.

4 Stir the filling and put 1 tablespoon in the bottom left-hand corner of the strip, about ¼-inch/5-mm from the short edge. Lift the corner over the filling to form a triangle so that the bottom edge now runs along the right-hand side. Fold the triangle upward, then to the left so that the open edges are across the top and the filling is enclosed. Continue folding the triangle from side to side, to the top. Dab the top with water and fold over to seal. Transfer to the baking sheet, seam-side down, and brush with butter. Repeat with the remaining sets of strips. Bake for 12–15 minutes, or until golden. Serve hot or at room temperature.

CAULIFLOWER, BROCCOLI & CASHEW SALAD

SERVES 4

INGREDIENTS

- 2 TBSP PEANUT OIL OR VEGETABLE OIL
- 2 RED ONIONS, CUT INTO WEDGES
- 1 SMALL HEAD CAULIFLOWER, CUT INTO FLORETS
- 1 SMALL HEAD BROCCOLI, CUT INTO FLORETS
- 2 TBSP PREPARED YELLOW CURRY PASTE OR RED CURRY PASTE
- 1¾ CUPS CANNED COCONUT MILK
- 1 TSP THAI FISH SAUCE
- 1 TSP JAGGERY
- 1 TSP SALT
- ½ CUP UNSALTED CASHEWS
- HANDFUL OF FRESH CILANTRO, CHOPPED, PLUS EXTRA SPRIGS, TORN, TO GARNISH

1 Heat the oil in a preheated wok. Add the onions and stir-fry over medium-high heat for 3–4 minutes, or until starting to brown. Add the cauliflower and broccoli and stir-fry for 1–2 minutes. Stir in the curry paste and stir-fry for 30 seconds, then add the coconut milk, fish sauce, jaggery, and salt. Bring gently to a boil, stirring occasionally, then reduce the heat and simmer gently for 3–4 minutes, or until the vegetables are almost tender.

2 Meanwhile, heat a separate dry skillet until hot. Add the cashews and cook, shaking the skillet frequently, for 2–3 minutes, or until lightly browned. Add to the stir-fry with the cilantro and stir well, then serve immediately, garnished with torn sprigs of cilantro.

SPINACH LASAGNE

SERVES 4

INGREDIENTS

- ½ CUP BUTTER, PLUS EXTRA FOR GREASING
- 2 GARLIC CLOVES, FINELY CHOPPED
- 4 OZ/115 G SHALLOTS
- 8 OZ/225 G WILD MUSHROOMS, SUCH AS CHANTERELLES
- 1 LB/450 G SPINACH, COOKED, DRAINED, AND FINELY CHOPPED
- 2 CUPS GRATED CHEDDAR CHEESE
- ¼ TSP FRESHLY GRATED NUTMEG
- 1 TSP CHOPPED FRESH BASIL
- SCANT ½ CUP ALL-PURPOSE FLOUR
- 2½ CUPS HOT MILK
- ⅔ CUP GRATED MILD HARD CHEESE
- 8 SHEETS PRECOOKED LASAGNE
- SALT AND PEPPER

1 Lightly grease a large ovenproof dish with a little butter and set aside.

2 Melt 4 tablespoons of the butter in a skillet. Add the garlic, shallots, and wild mushrooms and sauté over low heat, stirring frequently, for 3 minutes. Stir in the spinach, cheddar cheese, nutmeg, and basil. Season with salt and pepper to taste and set aside.

3 Melt the remaining butter in another skillet over low heat. Add the flour and cook, stirring constantly, for 1 minute. Gradually stir in the hot milk, whisking constantly until smooth. Stir in ¼ cup of the cheese and season to taste with salt and pepper.

4 Spread half of the mushroom and spinach mixture over the bottom of the prepared dish. Cover with a layer of half the lasagne sheets and then with half of the cheese sauce.

5 Repeat the layering process, then sprinkle over the remaining cheese.

6 Bake in a preheated oven, at 400°F/200°C, for about 30 minutes or until the topping is golden brown and bubbling. Serve hot straight from the dish.

STUFFED
CABBAGE ROLLS

SERVES 4

INGREDIENTS

- 8 LARGE OR 12 MEDIUM GREEN CABBAGE LEAVES
- 4 CUPS WATER
- ½ CUP PEARL BARLEY
- 2 TBSP CHOPPED FRESH PARSLEY
- 2 GARLIC CLOVES, COARSELY CHOPPED
- 4 CUPS CANNED CHOPPED TOMATOES
- 4 TBSP RED WINE VINEGAR
- 1 TBSP SUNFLOWER OIL OR CORN OIL, PLUS EXTRA FOR BRUSHING
- 2 ZUCCHINI, DICED
- 3 SCALLIONS, SLICED
- 2 TBSP BROWN SUGAR
- SALT AND GROUND BLACK PEPPER

1 Cut out the thick stems from the cabbage leaves, then blanch the leaves in a large saucepan of boiling water for 1 minute. Drain the leaves well and spread out to dry.

2 Bring the measured water to a boil in a large saucepan. Add the barley and half the chopped parsley, cover the pan, and simmer for 45 minutes, until the liquid has been absorbed.

3 Meanwhile, preheat the oven to 375°F/190°C. Put the garlic, 2 cups of tomatoes, and the vinegar in a blender or food processor and process to a smooth puree. Scrape into a bowl and set aside.

4 Heat the oil in a large skillet. Add the zucchini and the remaining parsley and cook, stirring frequently, for 3 minutes. Add the scallions and cook briefly, then add the tomato puree mixture. Cook for about 10 minutes, until thickened, then transfer to a large bowl.

5 Add the cooked barley to the bowl, season to taste, and stir well. Lightly brush an ovenproof dish with oil. Place a spoonful of the barley mixture at the stem end of a cabbage leaf. Roll up, tucking in the sides, and place, seam side down, in the dish. Stuff and roll the remaining cabbage leaves in the same way, placing them in the dish in a single layer.

6 Sprinkle the brown sugar over the cabbage rolls and pour the remaining tomatoes, with their can juice, on top. Cover with foil and bake in the preheated oven for 30 minutes, or until tender. Serve straight from the dish.

CAULIFLOWER & BROCCOLI TART

SERVES 4

INGREDIENTS

PIE DOUGH
- 1½ CUPS ALL-PURPOSE FLOUR, PLUS EXTRA FOR DUSTING
- PINCH OF SALT
- ½ TSP PAPRIKA
- 1 TSP DRIED THYME
- 6 TBSP MARGARINE
- 3 TBSP WATER

FILLING
- ¾ CUP CAULIFLOWER FLORETS
- 1 CUP BROCCOLI FLORETS
- 1 ONION, CUT INTO 8 WEDGES
- 2 TBSP BUTTER OR MARGARINE
- 1 TBSP ALL-PURPOSE FLOUR
- 6 TBSP VEGETABLE STOCK
- ½ CUP MILK
- ¾ CUP GRATED CHEDDAR CHEESE
- SALT AND PEPPER
- PAPRIKA, TO GARNISH

1 Preheat the oven to 375°F/190°C. To make the dough, sift the flour and salt into a bowl. Add the paprika and thyme and rub in the margarine. Stir in the water and bind to form a dough.

2 Roll out on a floured counter and line a 7-inch/18-cm loose-bottom tart pan. Prick the bottom and line with parchment paper. Fill with pie weights or dried beans and bake in the preheated oven, for 15 minutes. Remove the parchment and weights and return the pastry shell to the oven for 5 minutes.

3 To make the filling, cook the vegetables in a saucepan of lightly salted boiling water for 10–12 minutes, until tender. Drain and reserve.

4 Melt the butter in a saucepan. Add the flour and cook, stirring constantly, for 1 minute. Remove from the heat, stir in the stock and milk, and return to the heat. Bring to a boil, stirring constantly, and add ½ cup of the cheese. Season to taste with salt and pepper.

5 Spoon the cauliflower, broccoli, and onion into the pastry shell. Pour over the sauce and sprinkle with the remaining grated cheese. Return the tart to the oven for 10 minutes, until the cheese is golden and bubbling. Garnish with paprika and serve immediately.

CAULIFLOWER, EGGPLANT & GREEN BEAN KORMA

SERVES 4–6

INGREDIENTS

- SCANT ⅔ CUP CASHEWS
- 1½ TBSP GARLIC AND GINGER PASTE
- GENEROUS ¾ CUP WATER
- 4 TBSP GHEE, VEGETABLE OIL, OR PEANUT OIL
- 1 LARGE ONION, CHOPPED
- 5 GREEN CARDAMOM PODS, LIGHTLY CRUSHED
- 1 CINNAMON STICK, BROKEN IN HALF
- ¼ TSP GROUND TURMERIC
- GENEROUS 1 CUP HEAVY CREAM
- 5 OZ/140 G NEW POTATOES, SCRUBBED AND CHOPPED INTO ½-INCH/1-CM PIECES
- 5 OZ/140 G CAULIFLOWER FLORETS
- ½ TSP GARAM MASALA
- 5 OZ/140 G EGGPLANT, CHOPPED INTO CHUNKS
- 5 OZ/140 G GREEN BEANS, CHOPPED INTO ½-INCH/1-CM PIECES
- SALT AND PEPPER
- FRESH MINT OR CILANTRO, CHOPPED, TO GARNISH

1 Heat a large, flameproof casserole or skillet with a tight-fitting lid over high heat. Add the cashews and stir until they start to brown, then tip them out of the casserole into a spice blender. Add the garlic and ginger paste and 1 tablespoon of the water, and process until a coarse paste forms.

2 Melt the ghee in the casserole over medium–high heat. Add the onion and cook for 5–8 minutes, or until golden brown. Add the nut paste and stir for 5 minutes.

3 Stir in the cardamom pods, cinnamon stick, and turmeric. Add the cream and the remaining water and bring to a boil, stirring. Reduce the heat to the lowest level, cover the casserole, and simmer for 5 minutes.

4 Add the potatoes, cauliflower, and garam masala and simmer, covered, for 5 minutes. Stir in the eggplant and green beans and continue simmering for an additional 5 minutes, or until all the vegetables are tender. Check the sauce occasionally to make sure it isn't sticking on the bottom of the pan, and stir in extra water if needed.

5 Taste and add seasoning, if necessary. Sprinkle with the mint or cilantro to serve.

CHILE BROCCOLI
PASTA

SERVES 4

INGREDIENTS

- 2 CUPS DRY PENNE OR MACARONI
- 1 MEDIUM HEAD BROCCOLI
- ¼ CUP EXTRA VIRGIN OLIVE OIL
- 2 LARGE GARLIC CLOVES, CHOPPED
- 2 FRESH RED CHILES, SEEDED AND DICED
- 8 CHERRY TOMATOES (OPTIONAL)
- SMALL HANDFUL OF FRESH BASIL OR PARSLEY, TO GARNISH

1 Cook the penne or other pasta in a large saucepan of salted boiling water for about 10 minutes, until tender but still firm to the bite. Remove from the heat, drain, rinse with cold water, and drain again. Set aside.

2 Cut the broccoli into florets and cook in salted boiling water for 5 minutes. Drain, rinse with cold water, and drain again.

3 Heat the olive oil in the saucepan that the pasta was cooked in. Add the garlic and chiles, and tomatoes if using. Cook over high heat for 1 minute.

4 Return the broccoli to the pan with the oil and mix well. Cook for 2 minutes to heat through. Add the pasta and mix well again. Cook for 1 minute more.

5 Remove the pasta from the heat, turn into a large serving bowl, and serve garnished with basil or parsley.

SPINACH & RICOTTA GNOCCHI

SERVES 4–6

INGREDIENTS

- 1 TBSP OLIVE OIL
- 1 LB 2 OZ/500 G SPINACH LEAVES
- 1 CUP RICOTTA CHEESE
- 1 CUP FRESHLY GRATED PARMESAN OR ROMANO CHEESE
- 2 EGGS, LIGHTLY BEATEN
- GENEROUS ⅓ CUP ALL-PURPOSE FLOUR, PLUS EXTRA FOR DUSTING
- FRESHLY GRATED NUTMEG
- SALT AND PEPPER

SAUCE

- 2 TBSP OLIVE OIL
- 2 SHALLOTS, FINELY CHOPPED
- 1 CARROT, PEELED AND FINELY DICED
- 2 GARLIC CLOVES, CRUSHED
- 1 LB 12 OZ/800 G CANNED CHOPPED TOMATOES
- 1 TBSP TOMATO PASTE
- 6 FRESH BASIL LEAVES, COARSELY TORN INTO PIECES, PLUS EXTRA WHOLE FRESH BASIL LEAVES TO GARNISH

1 Heat the oil in a large saucepan. Add the spinach and cook, covered, for 1–2 minutes, or until just wilted. Drain through a colander and cool, then squeeze out as much water as possible with your hands (you can squeeze it in a clean dish towel to ensure that it is very dry.)

2 Finely chop the spinach and put in a bowl. Add the ricotta cheese, half the Parmesan cheese, the eggs, and flour, and mix well. Season to taste with salt and pepper and add a good grating of nutmeg. Cover and chill in the refrigerator for at least 1 hour.

3 Meanwhile, make the sauce. Heat the oil in a saucepan, then add the shallots, carrot, and garlic and cook over medium heat, stirring frequently, for 3–4 minutes, or until softened. Add the tomatoes and tomato paste and bring to a boil, then reduce the heat and simmer, uncovered, for 10–15 minutes, or until the sauce is reduced and thickened. Season to taste

with salt and pepper and add the basil leaves. If you like a smooth sauce, pass it through a strainer or process in a food processor or blender.

4 To shape the gnocchi, flour a plate and your hands thoroughly. Put a dessertspoonful of the spinach mixture into the palm of one hand, then roll gently into an egg shape and transfer to a floured baking sheet. Repeat with the remaining spinach mixture.

5 Bring a large saucepan of water to a simmer. Carefully add the gnocchi, in small batches, and cook gently for 2–3 minutes, or until they rise to the surface. Remove with a slotted spoon and transfer to a warmed serving dish to keep warm while you cook the remaining gnocchi.

6 Serve the gnocchi in warmed dishes with the sauce poured over the top and with the remaining Parmesan cheese to taste.

CABBAGE & WALNUT STIR-FRY

SERVES 4

INGREDIENTS

- 12 OZ/350 G WHITE CABBAGE
- 12 OZ/350 G RED CABBAGE
- 4 TBSP PEANUT OIL
- 1 TBSP WALNUT OIL
- 2 GARLIC CLOVES, CRUSHED
- 8 SCALLIONS, TRIMMED
- 8 OZ/225 G FIRM TOFU, CUBED
- 2 TBSP LEMON JUICE
- 1 CUP WALNUT HALVES
- 2 TSP DIJON MUSTARD
- 2 TSP POPPY SEEDS
- SALT AND PEPPER

1 Using a sharp knife, shred the white and red cabbages thinly and set aside until required.

2 Heat the peanut oil and walnut oil in a preheated wok. Add the garlic, cabbage, scallions, and tofu and cook for 5 minutes, stirring.

3 Add the lemon juice, walnuts, and mustard, season with salt and pepper, and cook for an additional 5 minutes, or until the cabbage is tender.

4 Transfer the stir-fry to a warm serving bowl, sprinkle with poppy seeds, and serve immediately.

BRUSSELS SPROUTS WITH CHESTNUTS

SERVES 4

INGREDIENTS
- 1 LB/450 G BRUSSELS SPROUTS
- ½ CUP UNSALTED BUTTER
- ¼ CUP BROWN SUGAR
- ½ CUP COOKED AND SHELLED CHESTNUTS
- SALT

1 Bring a large saucepan of salted water to a boil over high heat.

2 Trim the Brussels sprouts, removing the coarse stems and any loose outer leaves. Add to the pan of water and boil for 5–10 minutes, until just cooked but not too soft. Drain well, rinse in cold water, and drain again. Set aside.

3 Melt the butter in a heavy skillet. Add the sugar and stir over medium heat until dissolved.

4 Add the chestnuts to the skillet and cook, stirring occasionally, until they are well coated and starting to brown.

5 Add the sprouts to the skillet with the chestnuts and mix well. Reduce the heat and cook gently, stirring occasionally, for 3–4 minutes to heat through.

6 Remove from the heat, transfer to a serving dish, and serve immediately.

WATERCRESS, ZUCCHINI & MINT SALAD

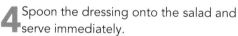

SERVES 4

INGREDIENTS

- 2 ZUCCHINI, CUT INTO BATONS
- 3½ OZ/100 G GREEN BEANS, CUT INTO THIRDS
- 1 GREEN BELL PEPPER, SEEDED AND CUT INTO STRIPS
- 2 CELERY STALKS, SLICED
- 1 BUNCH OF WATERCRESS
- SALT

DRESSING

- SCANT 1 CUP PLAIN YOGURT
- 1 GARLIC CLOVE, CRUSHED
- 2 TBSP CHOPPED FRESH MINT
- PEPPER

1 Bring a saucepan of lightly salted water to a boil, add the zucchini batons and beans, and cook for 7–8 minutes. Drain, rinse under cold running water, and drain again. Set aside to cool completely.

2 Mix the zucchini and beans with the bell pepper strips, celery, and watercress in a large serving bowl.

3 To make the dressing, combine the yogurt, garlic, and mint in a small bowl. Season with pepper to taste.

4 Spoon the dressing onto the salad and serve immediately.

BOK CHOY WITH CASHEWS

SERVES 4

INGREDIENTS

- 2 RED ONIONS
- 6 OZ/175 G RED CABBAGE
- 2 TBSP PEANUT OIL
- 8 OZ/225 G BOK CHOY
- 2 TBSP PLUM SAUCE
- SCANT 1 CUP ROASTED CASHEWS

1 Using a sharp knife, cut the red onions into thin wedges and thinly shred the red cabbage.

2 Put the peanut oil in a large preheated wok or heavy skillet and heat until it is really hot.

3 Add the onion wedges to the pan and stir-fry for about 5 minutes, or until the onions are just beginning to brown.

4 Add the red cabbage to the pan and stir-fry for an additional 2–3 minutes.

5 Add the bok choy leaves to the pan and stir-fry for about 5 minutes, or until the leaves have just wilted.

6 Drizzle the plum sauce over the vegetables, toss together until well combined, and heat until the liquid is beginning to bubble.

7 Sprinkle the roasted cashews over the stir-fry and transfer to warm serving bowls. Serve immediately.

RED CURRY WITH
MIXED LEAVES

SERVES 4

INGREDIENTS

- 2 TBSP PEANUT OIL OR VEGETABLE OIL
- 2 ONIONS, THINLY SLICED
- 1 BUNCH OF FINE ASPARAGUS SPEARS
- 1¾ CUPS CANNED COCONUT MILK
- 2 TBSP RED CURRY PASTE
- 3 FRESH KAFFIR LIME LEAVES
- 8 OZ/225 G BABY SPINACH LEAVES
- 2 HEADS BOK CHOY
- 1 SMALL HEAD CHINESE CABBAGE, SHREDDED
- HANDFUL OF FRESH CILANTRO, CHOPPED
- COOKED RICE, TO SERVE

1 Heat the oil in a preheated wok. Add the onions and asparagus and stir-fry over medium-high heat for 1–2 minutes.

2 Add the coconut milk, curry paste, and lime leaves and bring gently to a boil, stirring occasionally. Add the spinach, bok choy, and Chinese cabbage and cook, stirring, for 2–3 minutes, or until wilted. Add the cilantro and stir well. Serve immediately with rice.

ARUGULA & TOMATO RISOTTO

SERVES 4–6

INGREDIENTS

- 2 TBSP OLIVE OIL
- 2 TBSP UNSALTED BUTTER
- 1 LARGE ONION, FINELY CHOPPED
- 2 GARLIC CLOVES, FINELY CHOPPED
- 3 CUPS RISOTTO RICE
- ½ CUP DRY WHITE VERMOUTH
- 6⅓ CUPS VEGETABLE STOCK, SIMMERING
- 6 VINE-RIPENED OR ITALIAN PLUM TOMATOES, SEEDED AND CHOPPED
- 4½ OZ/125 G WILD ARUGULA
- HANDFUL OF FRESH BASIL LEAVES
- 1⅓ CUPS FRESHLY GRATED PARMESAN CHEESE
- 2 CUPS COARSELY GRATED OR DICED FRESH ITALIAN BUFFALO MOZZARELLA
- SALT AND PEPPER

1 Heat the oil and half the butter in a large skillet. Add the onion and cook for about 2 minutes, until just beginning to soften. Stir in the garlic and rice and cook, stirring frequently, until the rice is translucent and well coated.

2 Pour in the vermouth; it will evaporate almost immediately. Add a ladleful (about ½ cup) of the stock and cook, stirring, until it is absorbed.

3 Continue adding the stock, about half a ladleful at a time, allowing each addition to be absorbed before adding the next. Just before the rice is tender, stir in the chopped tomatoes and the arugula. Shred the basil leaves and immediately stir into the risotto. Continue to cook, adding more stock, until the risotto is creamy and the rice is tender but still firm to the bite.

4 Remove from the heat and stir in the remaining butter, the grated Parmesan, and mozzarella. Season to taste with salt and pepper. Remove the pan from the heat, cover, and let the risotto stand for about 1 minute. Serve immediately, before the mozzarella melts completely.

additives 19
albumen 19
alcohol 19
almonds 150
  avocado & almond soup 80
  chilled garlic soup 142
  nutty bleu cheese roast 180
antioxidants 12
apples 23
  sweet potato & apple soup 44
artichokes 20
  artichoke & pimiento flatbread 50
arugula 21
  arugula & tomato risotto 220
asparagus 20, 42
  asparagus & sun-dried tomato risotto 68
  asparagus with sweet tomato dressing 67
  red curry with mixed leaves 219
avocados 20, 78-9
  avocado & almond soup 80
  chili tofu tortillas 98
  guacamole 82

bananas 25
barley 27
  stuffed cabbage rolls 201
basil 30
  arugula & tomato risotto 220
  nutty bleu cheese roast 180
  pasta salad with charbroiled bell peppers 92
  pesto sauce 37
  zucchini & basil risotto 94
  see also pesto
bay 30
bean sprouts 20
  bean sprout salad 70
  stir-fried bean sprouts 73
  vegetable & black bean spring rolls 162
beans 153
  cooking 153
beets 20, 43
  beet salad 46
bell peppers 20, 78
  bean sprout salad 70
  bell peppers with feta 88
  cashew paella 183
  chili tofu tortillas 98
  eggplant curry 109
  kidney bean risotto 172
  nutty bleu cheese roast 180
  Parmesan cheese risotto with mushrooms 122
  pasta salad with charbroiled bell peppers 92
  vegetable & black bean spring rolls 162
  watercress, zucchini & mint salad 214
  zucchini & basil risotto 94
  see also pimientos
black currants 23
blackberries 24, 25
blueberries 24
bok choy 21, 189
  bok choy with cashews 216
  red curry with mixed leaves 219
borlotti beans 153
  saucy borlotti beans 168
brassicas and leafy greens 21, 188-9
bread
  artichoke & pimiento flatbread 50
  chilled garlic soup 142
  cornmeal with tomatoes & garlic sauce 110
  flatbread with onion & rosemary 128
  hummus toasts with olives 159
  roast garlic with goat cheese 145
  tomato & rosemary focaccia 86
  traditional bean & cabbage soup 192
  wild mushroom bruschetta 118
broccoli 21, 188
  broccoli & cheese soup 190

cauliflower & broccoli tart 202
cauliflower, broccoli & cashew salad 196
chile broccoli pasta 207
Brussels sprouts 21, 188
  Brussels sprouts with chestnuts 213
bulgur wheat, chickpea & vegetable stew 160
butternut squash 20, 79
  butternut squash stir-fry 104
  roasted root vegetables 62

cabbage 21, 188
  bok choy with cashews 216
  cabbage & walnut stir-fry 210
  stuffed cabbage rolls 201
  traditional bean & cabbage soup 192
  see also Chinese cabbage
cannellini beans 153
  traditional bean & cabbage soup 192
capers: potato gnocchi with walnut pesto 52
carbohydrates 14, 18
cardamom 31
  cauliflower, eggplant & green bean korma 204
carrots 20, 43
  avocado & almond soup 80
  bean sprout salad 70
  carrot & orange stir-fry 55
  chickpea & vegetable stew 160
  roasted root vegetables 62
  sweet potato & apple soup 44
  traditional bean & cabbage soup 192
  vegetable & black bean spring rolls 162
cashews 150
  bok choy with cashews 216
  butternut squash stir-fry 104
  cashew paella 183
  cauliflower, broccoli & cashew salad 196
  cauliflower, eggplant & green bean korma 204
  kidney bean risotto 172
cauliflower 21, 188
  cauliflower & broccoli tart 202
  cauliflower, broccoli & cashew salad 196
  cauliflower, eggplant & green bean korma 204
cayenne pepper 31
celeriac 43
celery 42
  avocado & almond soup 80
  baked celery with cream 64
  bean sprout salad 70
  bleu cheese & walnut tartlets 184
  chickpea & vegetable stew 160
  kidney bean risotto 172
  nutty bleu cheese roast 180
  Parmesan cheese risotto with mushrooms 122
  traditional bean & cabbage soup 192
  watercress, zucchini & mint salad 214
chard 189
cheese 19, 29
  arugula & tomato risotto 220
  bleu cheese & walnut tartlets 184
  broccoli & cheese soup 190
  caramelized onion tart 130
  cauliflower & broccoli tart 202
  cheese sauce 36
  chili tofu tortillas 98
  mixed mushroom pizza 124
  nutty bleu cheese roast 180
  spinach & ricotta gnocchi 208
  spinach lasagne 198
  stuffed eggplants 106
  see also feta cheese; goat cheese; Parmesan cheese
cherries 23
chestnuts 150
  Brussels sprouts with chestnuts 213
  nutty bleu cheese roast 180
  pumpkin chesnut risotto 103
chickpeas 153

chickpea & vegetable stew 160
chickpea soup 156
hummus toasts with olives 159
chicory 21, 42
chiles 78
  cashew paella 183
  chile broccoli pasta 207
  chili tofu tortillas 98
  Egyptian brown beans 171
  guacamole 82
  onion dal 134
  pasta all'arrabbiata 97
  sesame hot noodles 177
Chinese cabbage 188
  leeks with yellow bean sauce 140
  red curry with mixed leaves 219
chives 30
  chickpea & vegetable stew 160
  cornmeal with tomatoes & garlic sauce 110
  leek & goat cheese crêpes 136
cilantro 30
  butternut squash stir-fry 104
  cauliflower, broccoli & cashew salad 196
  eggplant curry 109
  green bean salad with feta 174
  guacamole 82
  potato fritters with onion & tomato relish 49
  red curry with mixed leaves 219
  sesame hot noodles 177
cinnamon 31
citrus fruit 22
  segmenting 23
cloves 31
coconut 151
  butternut squash stir-fry 104
  cauliflower, broccoli & cashew salad 196
  eggplant curry 109
  red curry with mixed leaves 219
cooking techniques and timings 32-4
coriander 31
  baked celery with cream 64
  butternut squash stir-fry 104
  potato fritters with onion & tomato relish 49
corn 27
  cashew paella 183
  leeks with yellow bean sauce 140
  potato fritters with onion & tomato relish 49
cornmeal with tomatoes & garlic sauce 110
cream 28
  baked celery with cream 64
  bleu cheese & walnut tartlets 184
  caramelized onion tart 130
  cauliflower, eggplant & green bean korma 204
  mushroom pasta with port 121
  pasta shapes with pumpkin sauce 100
  sweet potato & apple soup 44
cucumbers 20, 79
  bean sprout salad 70
  cucumber & tomato soup 85
  tzatziki 38
  vegetable & black bean spring rolls 162
cumin 31
  baked celery with cream 64
  butternut squash stir-fry 104
  potato fritters with onion & tomato relish 49

dairy produce 28-9
  nondairy alternatives 28
dal: onion dal 134
dill 30
  fava beans with feta 166
  spinach & feta triangles 195

dough: see pie dough
eggplants 20, 78
  cauliflower, eggplant & green bean korma 204
  eggplant curry 109

stuffed eggplants 106
eggs 19
    bleu cheese & walnut tartlets 184
    caramelized onion tart 130
    leek & herb soufflés 139
    spinach & ricotta gnocchi 208
    tomato & potato tortilla 91

fats, dietary 12, 15, 19
fava beans
    Egyptian brown beans 171
    fava beans with feta 166
fennel 20, 42
    fennel risotto with vodka 74
feta cheese 29
    bell peppers with feta 88
    fava beans with feta 166
    green bean salad with feta 174
    spinach & feta triangles 195
    see also cheese; goat cheese; Parmesan
        cheese
fiber 12, 18
food hygiene 13
fruits 22-5
fruit vegetables 78

garlic 21, 115
    artichoke & pimiento flatbread 50
    arugula & tomato risotto 220
    avocado & almond soup 80
    baked celery with cream 64
    bean sprout salad 70
    beet salad 46
    butternut squash stir-fry 104
    cabbage & walnut stir-fry 210
    cashew paella 183
    chickpea soup 156
    chickpea & vegetable stew 160
    chile broccoli pasta 207
    chili tofu tortillas 98
    chilled garlic soup 142
    cornmeal with tomatoes & garlic sauce 110
    eggplant curry 109
    garlic mash potatoes 56
    garlic spaghetti 146
    hummus toasts with olives 159
    kidney bean risotto 172
    mixed mushroom pizza 124
    nutty bleu cheese roast 180
    onion dal 134
    Parmesan cheese risotto with mushrooms 122
    pasta all'arrabbiata 97
    potato fritters with onion & tomato relish 49
    potato gnocchi with walnut pesto 52
    roast garlic with goat cheese 145
    roasted potato wedges with shallots &
        rosemary 58
    roasted root vegetables 62
    stuffed eggplants 106
    traditional bean & cabbage soup 192
    tzatziki 38
    wild mushroom bruschetta 118
    zucchini & basil risotto 94
gelatin 19
ginger 31
    onion dal 134
    vegetable & black bean spring rolls 162
globe artichokes 42
goat cheese
    leek & goat cheese crêpes 136
    roast garlic with goat cheese 145
    see also cheese; feta cheese; goat cheese
gooseberries 24
grapes 24
gravy 19
green beans
    cauliflower, eggplant & green bean korma 204

green bean salad with feta 174
    watercress, zucchini & mint salad 214
guacamole 82

herbs 30
    freezing 31

Jerusalem artichokes 43

kidney beans 153
    bean burgers 165
    kidney bean risotto 172
kiwis 25

leeks 21
    bleu cheese & walnut tartlets 184
    carrot & orange stir-fry 55
    chickpea & vegetable stew 160
    leek & goat cheese crêpes 136
    leek & herb soufflés 139
    leeks with yellow bean sauce 140
    sweet potato & apple soup 44
lemons 22
    avocado & almond soup 80
    Egyptian brown beans 171
    fava beans with feta 166
    fennel risotto with vodka 74
    hummus toasts with olives 159
    pasta salad with charbroiled bell peppers 92
lentils 152
    onion dal 134
lettuce 21, 189
limes 22
    chili tofu tortillas 98
    guacamole 82
    sesame hot noodles 177

mangoes 25
margarine 19
mayonnaise 37
meal planning 18-19
melons 24
    cucumber & tomato soup 85
milk 28
millet 27
mint 30
    cucumber & tomato soup 85
    potato fritters with onion & tomato relish 49
    tzatziki 38
    watercress, zucchini & mint salad 214
mushrooms 21, 115
    bean burgers 165
    creamy mushroom & tarragon soup 116
    kidney bean risotto 172
    mixed mushroom pizza 124
    mushroom pasta with port 121
    Parmesan cheese risotto with mushrooms 122
    spinach lasagne 198
    wild mushroom bruschetta 118

nectarines 23
noodles: sesame hot noodles 177
nutmeg 31
    sweet potato & apple soup 44
nuts 150-1
    nutty bleu cheese roast 180
    toasting 151
    see also almonds; cashews; chestnuts; peanuts;
    walnuts

oats 27
olives
    artichoke & pimiento flatbread 50
    cashew paella 183
onions 21, 115
    artichoke & pimiento flatbread 50
    arugula & tomato risotto 220

asparagus & sun-dried tomato risotto 68
avocado & almond soup 80
baked celery with cream 64
bean burgers 165
beet salad 46
bok choy with cashews 216
broccoli & cheese soup 190
butternut squash stir-fry 104
caramelized onion tart 130
cashew paella 183
cauliflower & broccoli tart 202
cauliflower, broccoli & cashew salad 196
cauliflower, eggplant & green bean korma 204
chickpea soup 156
chickpea & vegetable stew 160
chili tofu tortillas 98
creamy mushroom & tarragon soup 116
Egyptian brown beans 171
fennel risotto with vodka 74
flatbread with onion & rosemary 128
green bean salad with feta 174
kidney bean risotto 172
mushroom pasta with port 121
nutty bleu cheese roast 180
Parmesan cheese risotto with mushrooms 122
pasta shapes with pumpkin sauce 100
potato fritters with onion & tomato relish 49
pumpkin chestnut risotto 103
red curry with mixed leaves 219
red onion, tomato & herb salad 127
roasted potato wedges with shallots &
    rosemary 58
saucy borlotti beans 168
stuffed eggplants 106
traditional bean & cabbage soup 192
vegetable cakes 133
wild mushroom bruschetta 118
zucchini & basil risotto 94
see also scallions
oranges 22
    caramelized sweet potatoes 61
    carrot & orange stir-fry 55
oregano 30
    green bean salad with feta 174
    mixed mushroom pizza 124
    Parmesan cheese risotto with mushrooms 122
    stuffed eggplants 106

papayas 25
paprika 31
    chili tofu tortillas 98
Parmesan cheese
    arugula & tomato risotto 220
    asparagus & sun-dried tomato risotto 68
    asparagus with sweet tomato dressing 67
    baked celery with cream 64
    fennel risotto with vodka 74
    mixed mushroom pizza 124
    Parmesan cheese risotto with mushrooms 122
    pasta with pesto 178
    pasta shapes with pumpkin sauce 100
    pesto sauce 37
    potato gnocchi with walnut pesto 52
    pumpkin chestnut risotto 103
    see also cheese; feta cheese; goat cheese
parsley 30
    bean burgers 165
    broccoli & cheese soup 190
    cashew paella 183
    chili tofu tortillas 98
    cornmeal with tomatoes & garlic sauce 110
    garlic spaghetti 146
    kidney bean risotto 172
    pasta all'arrabbiata 97
    pasta shapes with pumpkin sauce 100

potato gnocchi with walnut pesto 52
stuffed cabbage rolls 201
tomato & potato tortilla 91
traditional bean & cabbage soup 192
parsnips: roasted root vegetables 62
passion fruits 25
pasta
chile broccoli pasta 207
garlic spaghetti 146
mushroom pasta with port 121
pasta all'arrabbiata 97
pasta salad with charbroiled bell peppers 92
pasta shapes with pumpkin sauce 100
pasta with pesto 178
spinach lasagne 198
stuffed eggplants 106
peaches 23
peanuts
carrot & orange stir-dry 55
sesame hot noodles 177
pears 23
peas
cashew paella 183
chilled pea soup 154
peas, dried 152
pepper 31
pesto
pasta salad with charbroiled bell peppers 92
pesto sauce 37
pasta with pesto 178
pie dough
flaky pie dough 38
pizza dough 39
puff pie dough 39
pimientos: artichoke & pimiento flatbread 50
pine nuts 150
asparagus with sweet tomato dressing 67
pasta with pesto 178
pesto sauce 37
spinach & feta triangles 195
pineapples 25
caramelized sweet potatoes 61
pinto beans: bean burgers 165
pizza
mixed mushroom pizza 124
pizza dough 39
plums 23
potatoes 20, 43
broccoli & cheese soup 190
cauliflower, eggplant & green bean korma 204
garlic mash potatoes 56
potato fritters with onion & tomato relish 49
potato gnocchi with walnut pesto 52
roasted potato wedges with shallots & rosemary 58
tomato & potato tortilla 91
vegetable cakes 133
protein 14, 18
pumpkins 20, 79
pasta shapes with pumpkin sauce 100
pumpkin chesnut risotto 103

quinoa 27

raspberries 24
red currants 23
rice 27
arugula & tomato risotto 220
asparagus & sun-dried tomato risotto 68
cashew paella 183
cooked rice, storing and reusing 26
fennel risotto with vodka 74

kidney bean risotto 172
Parmesan cheese risotto with mushrooms 122
pumpkin chesnut risotto 103
zucchini & basil risotto 94
roots, shoots & stems 20, 42-3
rosemary 30
flatbread with onion & rosemary 128
roast garlic with goat cheese 145
roasted potato wedges with shallots & rosemary 58
roasted root vegetables 62
tomato & rosemary focaccia 86
rye 27

saffron 31
pumpkin chesnut risotto 103
sage 30
roasted root vegetables 62
saucy borlotti beans 168
salad greens 189
scallions 21
beet salad 46
cabbage & walnut stir-fry 210
chilled pea soup 154
cucumber & tomato soup 85
eggplant curry 109
leeks with yellow bean sauce 140
onion dal 134
potato fritters with onion & tomato relish 49
spinach & feta triangles 195
stir-fried bean sprouts 73
tomato & potato tortilla 91
vegetable & black bean spring rolls 162
see also onions
seeds 151
toasting 151
serving sizes 14
sesame seeds 151
sesame hot noodles 177
sour cream
chili tofu tortillas 98
creamy mushroom & tarragon soup 116
soybeans 153
spices 31
spinach 21, 189
red curry with mixed leaves 219
spinach & feta triangles 195
spinach & ricotta gnocchi 208
spinach lasagne 198
squashes 20, 79
strawberries 24
suet 19
sweet potatoes 20, 43
caramelized sweet potatoes 61
roasted root vegetables 62
sweet potato & apple soup 44
Swiss chard 189
chickpea soup 156

tarragon 30
creamy mushroom & tarragon soup 116
thyme 30
roasted root vegetables 62
tofu 28, 153
cabbage & walnut stir-fry 210
chili tofu tortillas 98
tomatoes 20, 78
arugula & tomato risotto 220
asparagus & sun-dried tomato risotto 68
asparagus with sweet tomato dressing 67
bean sprout salad 70
cashew paella 183

chickpea & vegetable stew 160
chickpea soup 156
chile broccoli pasta 207
chili tofu tortillas 98
cornmeal with tomatoes & garlic sauce 110
cucumber & tomato soup 85
Egyptian brown beans 171
green bean salad with feta 174
guacamole 82
mushroom pasta with port, cream 121
Parmesan cheese risotto with mushrooms 122
pasta all'arrabbiata 97
potato fritters with onion & tomato relish 49
red onion, tomato & herb salad 127
saucy borlotti beans 168
spinach & ricotta gnocchi 208
stuffed cabbage rolls 201
stuffed eggplants 106
tomato & potato tortilla 91
tomato & rosemary focaccia 86
tomato sauce 37
traditional bean & cabbage soup 192
turnips
chickpea & vegetable stew 160
roasted root vegetables 62
tzatziki 38

vanilla 31
vegetable fruits 20
vegetable stock 36
vegetarian diet 10
balanced diet 14-15, 18
changing to 10
for children 18
demi-veg 10
food hygiene 13
fruitarian 10
health benefits 12-13
lacto-ovo-vegetarian 10
lacto-vegetarian 10
lifestyle choice 13
macrobiotic vegetarian 10
meal planning 18-19
religious choice 12
vegan 10, 15, 28
vitamins and minerals 15, 16-17

walnuts 151
bleu cheese & walnut tartlets 184
cabbage & walnut stir-fry 210
cornmeal with tomatoes & garlic sauce 110
leek & herb soufflés 139
potato gnocchi with walnut pesto 52
water chestnuts: vegetable & black bean spring rolls 162
watercress 21
watercress, zucchini & mint salad 214
white currants 23

yogurt 28
chilled pea soup 154
tzatziki 38
watercress, zucchini & mint salad 214

zucchini 20, 79
eggplant curry 109
nutty bleu cheese roast 180
stuffed cabbage rolls 201
watercress, zucchini & mint salad 214
zucchini & basil risotto 94